Multiplying Servant Leaders

A Training Manual for Facilitators

MULTIPLYING SERVANT LEADERS: A TRAINING MANUAL FOR FACILITATORS

© 2018 BEE World

Every attempt has been made to provide correct information. However, the publisher does not guarantee the accuracy of the book and does not assume responsibility for information included in or omitted from it.

All scripture quotations, unless otherwise indicated, are taken from the NET Bible®, ©1996-2006 by Biblical Studies Press, L.L.C. www.bible.org. All rights reserved. This material is available in its entirety as a free download or online web use at http://net.bible.org. Scripture quotations marked as NASB are taken from the New American Standard Bible, © 1960, 1995 by The Lockman Foundation. Used by permission. Scripture quotations marked KJV are taken from the King James Version.

All rights reserved. This publication is protected by copyright, and except for brief excerpts for review purposes, permission must be obtained from the publisher prior to any prohibited reproduction, storage in a retrieval system, or transmission in any form or by any means, electronic, mechanical, photocopying, recording, or likewise.

For information regarding permissions or special orders, please contact:

BEE World
International Headquarters
990 Pinon Ranch View, Ste. 100
Colorado Springs, CO 80907

ISBN: 978-1-937324-30-8

First Edition

Printed in the United States of America

1 2 3 4 5 6 7 8 9 10

08012018

Contents

INTRODUCTION 1
UNIT 1: LEADING THROUGH SERVING 5
LESSON 1: WHAT IS A SERVANT LEADER? 7
    Topic 1: The Teachings and Example of Jesus 7
    Topic 2: Combining Service with Leadership 9
    Topic 3: Becoming a Servant Leader 11
Lesson 1 Answers to Questions 13
LESSON 2: WHAT ARE THE PERSONAL QUALITIES OF A SERVANT LEADER? ... 15
    Topic 1: Devotion to God 16
    Topic 2: Quality of Character 16
    Topic 3: Manner of Speaking 17
    Topic 4: Vision for Multiplying Disciples 17
    Topic 5: Managing Time 18
LESSON 3: HOW ARE SERVANT LEADERS DEVELOPED? 19
    Topic 1: The Training Method: Facilitated, Interactive Learning 19
    Topic 2: The Training Process: Three Phases of Development 20
UNIT 2: FACILITATING COURSES 23
LESSON 4: TEACHING INTERACTIVELY 25
    Topic 1: How Jesus Taught and Trained His Disciples 25
    Topic 2: How the Apostle Paul Developed Servant leaders for the New Testament Church 26
    Topic 3: How We Can Develop Servant Leaders Today 27
LESSON 5: THE COURSE WORKBOOK 29
    Topic 1: Design of the Course Workbook 29
    Topic 2: Structure of the Course Workbook 30
LESSON 6: USING QUESTIONS TO FACILITATE LEARNING 33
    Topic 1: Jesus, Master Questioner 33
    Topic 2: Introductory Questions 34
    Topic 3: Inductive Study Questions 35
    Topic 4: Follow-Up Questions 38
    Topic 5: Evaluating Questions 39
LESSON 7: USING CREATIVE LEARNING ACTIVITIES 43
    Topic 1: Creative Facilitating 43
    Topic 2: Team Facilitating 45
    Topic 3: Student Involvement 46
    Topic 4: Short Lecture 46
    Topic 5: Guidelines for Effective Use of Creative Learning Activities 47
LESSON 8: WRITING LESSON PLANS 49
    Topic 1: Why is Lesson Planning Important? 49
    Topic 2: An Overview of a Good Lesson Plan 50
    Topic 3: A Step-by-step Guide to Writing a Targeted Lesson Plan 51
LESSON 9: LEARNING TO LEAD A SMALL GROUP TRAINING SESSION 55
    Topic 1: Describing the Small Group 56
    Topic 2: Leading a Small Group 56
    Topic 3: Managing Common Problem Areas 57
    Topic 4: Evaluating the Small Group 58

UNIT THREE: TRAINING OTHERS 61
LESSON 10: PREPARING AN EFFECTIVE TRAINING PLAN 63
Topic 1: Why You Must Have a Plan for Training Servant Leaders 64
Topic 2: The Critical Components of an Effective Plan for Training Servant Leaders 64
Topic 3: How Training Servant Leaders Relates to Other Ministries of the Church 66
LESSON 11: CHOOSING THE RIGHT STUDENTS 69
Topic 1: Characteristics of the Ideal BEE Student 69
Topic 2: Test Ability and Commitment 70
Topic 3: Understand the Context and Vision for the Training 71
LESSON 12: IMPLEMENTING YOUR TRAINING PLAN (STARTING YOUR GROUP) 73
Topic 1: Planning for a Training Event 73
Topic 2: Facilitating the First Training Event 74
Topic 3: Facilitating a Course to Completion 76
Topic 4: Mentoring Your Students 77
LESSON 13: EVALUATING THE EFFECTIVENESS OF YOUR TRAINING 79
Topic 1: Guidelines for Evaluating Your Training 79
Topic 2: Gathering and Making Reports 80
Topic 3: Solving Common Problem Areas 80

UNIT FOUR: MENTORING FOR MULTIPLICATION 83
LESSON 14: HELPING YOUR STUDENTS CATCH A VISION FOR MULTIPLICATION 85
Topic 1: Modeling Multiplication 85
Topic 2: Communicating a Vision for Multiplication 86
Topic 3: Making Your Vision Take Root 87
LESSON 15: HELPING YOUR STUDENTS START NEW GROUPS 89
Topic 1: Preparing Your Students to Begin Their Own Groups 90
Topic 2: Partnering with Your Students to Start New Groups 91
Topic 3: Supporting Your Students Through the Process of Starting New Groups 93
Topic 4: Releasing Your Students to Lead Their Groups 96
LESSON 16: ENTRUSTING THE MINISTRY TO THOSE YOU HAVE TRAINED 103
Topic 1: How Jesus Entrusted the Ministry to Those He Trained 103
Topic 2: How the Apostle Paul Entrusted the Ministry to Those He Trained 106
Topic 3: How We Can Entrust the Ministry to Those We Have Trained 110

APPENDIX 1: BEE WORLD CORE VALUES 117
APPENDIX 2: EDUCATIONAL METHODOLOGY 119
APPENDIX 3: TIME IN A JAR ILLUSTRATION 121
APPENDIX 4: PAPER PEOPLE ACTIVITY 125
APPENDIX 5: A SAMPLE LESSON PLAN 127
APPENDIX 6: BEE CURRICULUM 129
APPENDIX 7: SUGGESTED TRAINING SCHEDULES 131
APPENDIX 8: A SAMPLE TRAINING PLAN AND TEMPLATE 133
APPENDIX 9: EVALUATING YOUR TRAINING 137
APPENDIX 10: REPORT FORMS AND LINKS 139

Introduction

The Need of the Church for Leaders

One of the greatest needs of the church around the world is for godly, trained leaders—men and women who understand what God wants them to be and do, who are biblically trained, and who have the passion and courage to carry out the vision God has given them.

Biblical Mandates for the Church

The Bible is very clear as to what the church should be doing. The primary goal is to make disciples.

Jesus' final instructions to the twelve whom He had personally trained was "Go make disciples" (Matt 28:19). In Colossians 1:28-29 the Apostle Paul reminds us that the task of making disciples is to help every Christian become "complete in Christ," that is, spiritually mature. Spiritual maturity does not happen overnight but requires progress over time as one applies biblical truth to his or her life. This implies accountability and careful oversight, with older and more mature believers helping younger ones.

Partnering with the Local Church to Provide Ongoing Training

We exist to serve the church around the world by providing the training that is essential for fulfilling the biblical mandates listed above. We do this in partnership with local churches and church-planting agencies. Our goal is not to take trained Christian workers away from the local church, but to help train and mobilize church members so that the local church can be better prepared to carry out its mission. The BEE strategy is church-based, not school campus-based. Therefore, students do not have to leave their community and church involvement to pursue a degree. Rather, they remain in their cultural context and continue to minister in their local church environment while they receive and learn to pass on the biblical and practical training BEE provides.

How does it work? Qualified students who have been recommended by their church and accepted by BEE are organized into a small group with other students to study through the course materials made available by BEE. As they study, they are also trained to use these materials to train others.

The BEE Approach to Learning

One important distinctive of BEE is its approach to learning. Rather than relying on the traditional method of lecture by a teacher, our learning style is focused on guided group interaction. We use the term "facilitation" to describe this type of learning. A study group usually consists of approximately 12-16 students. Each student is responsible for working through the assigned lesson in the course materials prior to the start of a facilitation session. When the group comes together, a team of facilitators leads the group in interaction about what they have studied. Not only is this more stimulating to the students, but because the process does not require an expert teacher, the students learn how they can do the same thing later with groups of their own. This is an extremely important concept for the sake of multiplication.

Spiritual Multiplication Is the Key

In 2 Timothy 2:2, we see the multiplication strategy the Apostle Paul employed. He trained Timothy (among others) and instructed him to entrust the Word he had been taught to faithful men who would be able to teach others also.

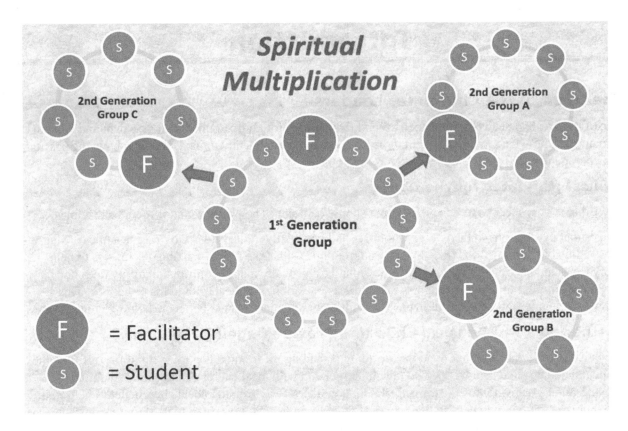

The faithful men and women in BEE study groups are entrusted with biblical truths, so that they will be ABLE TO TEACH OTHERS ALSO. This is the principle of spiritual multiplication. Learning is not an end in itself but must be seen as an entrustment by God for the purpose of being able to train others. Hence, it is crucial that the students in a BEE study group (Generation 1) go on to be facilitators of their own groups (Generation 2), and that those in these groups in turn start their own groups (Generation 3). If done well, this strategy will result in leaders being multiplied through many generations.

BEE Learning Objectives: Know, Be, Do

Often in educational situations, even in the church, the goal is nothing more than the memorization of information, as though the accumulation of knowledge was the goal. Changed lives should be the goal of biblical training (Rom 12:1-2). Certainly, this rests on a foundation of knowing biblical truth, yet such knowledge must lead to transformation of mind and character. A true disciple will not only *know* the Word of God; he will also *be* the person the Lord wants him to be.

Finally, we are to *do* something with what we have received. We are to serve the Lord according to the gifts He has given each one of us. Every Christian is responsible to skillfully use the gifts he has been given to make disciples. BEE courses are designed to develop critical ministry skills, thus enabling the students to competently carry out the ministry God has entrusted to them.

In all the courses we offer, these three important aspects—knowing, being, and doing—are continually emphasized. Application of the Word of God to life is built into every course.

Objectives of This Manual
- To equip faithful men and women to lead by serving
- To build the confidence, understanding, and skills of these "servant leaders," that they might be able to effectively facilitate BEE courses, train facilitators, and mentor others toward multiplication of the training
- To provide these servant leaders with a resource handbook

Course Description

This manual includes four Units:

Unit 1: Leading Through Serving is an introduction to what it means to lead through serving—how one can become a servant leader, and how one who is becoming a servant leader can help others to follow him, as he follows Christ.

Unit 2: Facilitating Courses is a step-by-step guide to facilitating BEE courses, with exercises to help each student develop the critical skills required.

Unit 3: Training Others is a step-by-step guide to training others to facilitate BEE courses.

Unit 4: Mentoring for Multiplication gives instruction in how to come alongside those you train to help them establish their own system for multiplying servant leaders through multiple generations.

Lesson Organization

Each lesson is divided into the following parts: Title, Introduction, Objectives, Outline, Topics, Questions, and Exercises.

- The title, introduction, objectives, and outline provide a preview of the lesson.
- Topics are used to develop the lesson objectives.
- Questions will help the student understand and reflect on the truths taught in the lesson.
- Exercises will help the student apply the lesson their lives and ministries.

Student Instructions

How to use this manual: This manual is not a stand-alone course. It is designed to be used in conjunction with other BEE courses throughout the entire process of developing a multiplying training system. Both trainers and trainees will find it helpful to frequently refer to and use this manual as they together move through the training process.

Exercises: The exercises are designed to help the facilitator apply the lesson content and fulfill the objectives. Generally, they are made up of a series of questions to be first personally answered, and then discussed in the context of a small group.

> **Important Instruction for Facilitators Concerning Scope and Sequence**
>
> Make sure every BEE student receives a copy of this manual at the beginning of the training program and stress the importance of their bringing it with them to every training session.
>
> Provide an orientation to the contents of the manual at the first training session and assign the reading of the entire manual prior to the second session.
>
> At the second training session answer any questions your students have about the whole training process, and work with them through the Introduction and Unit 1.
>
> At succeeding sessions, work through the rest of the manual, in order, with your students as they progress through the training program.
>
> Review the contents of lessons already covered as needed.

Materials needed: In addition to this manual, you will need your Bible, a BEE course that each member in the group has studied, and a notebook to write down your answers to the practical assignments.

Study with another person: If you are not part of a small group of students studying the BEE courses try to find at least one other person to work through this course material with you.

Tests and grades: The test for this course is not on paper, but in the real world, written in the lives of those you impact for the Kingdom of God. Application of the principles of this course in your ministry, as demonstrated by the establishment of a second-generation group (at a minimum), is a requirement for graduation from the BEE training program.

Unit 1: Leading Through Serving

Unit Introduction

This unit lays the foundation for the challenging adventure of developing servant leaders for the church. Three important questions will be answered:1) What is a servant leader? 2) What are the personal qualities of a servant leader? 3) How are servant leaders developed?

In Lesson 1, we will seek to understand what kind of leaders God wants us to be and reproduce. Then in Lesson 2, we will be challenged to evaluate personal areas that influence our effectiveness as servant leaders. Finally, in Lesson 3, we will examine the process of becoming and helping others become servant leaders.

Unit Objectives

- To establish the foundational importance of those who would lead the church of God seeing themselves first as servants of Christ and His church.
- To identify the personal qualities necessary to become a servant leader.
- To understand the major responsibilities, we must undertake and faithfully carry out if we are to become and help others become servant leaders.

Unit Outline

Lesson 1: What Is a Servant leader?

Lesson 2: What are the Personal Qualities of a Servant leader?

Lesson 3: How are Servant Leaders Developed?

Lesson 1: What is a Servant Leader?

"...whoever wants to be great among you must be your servant...."
— Mark 10:45

Much has been written about servant leadership, so much, in fact, that it is difficult to know what the term means. For many, the term merely denotes a style of leadership, one that is kinder, gentler, more participative. Some, especially in the marketplace, use it in something of a manipulative manner. They suggest that leaders should serve others, so they will produce more. The emphasis often seems to be primarily on leadership, with serving being something a leader does. That is not the biblical idea of servant leadership. Leadership is important, but servanthood is foundational. We believe that God is seeking to raise up servants to lead His church, rather than leaders who serve their churches. It may seem at first to be too fine a distinction, but, as you will discover in this lesson, there is a significant difference.

Key concept: Those who would lead Christ's church must see themselves as servants of Christ who are called to serve others in the role of leader.

Objectives

As a result of studying this lesson, you will:

- Be able to explain the biblical basis for leading as servants
- Be motivated to develop and maintain a servant heart as you lead
- Respond by evaluating your leadership philosophy and practice with a view to making these conform more closely to the servant leader pattern given us in the Bible

Outline

Topic 1: The Teachings and Example of Jesus

Topic 2: Combining Service with Leadership

Topic 3: Becoming a Servant leader

Topic 1: The Teachings and Example of Jesus

Jesus sets the standard for what it means to be a servant leader both by His example and by His teachings. Prior to his incarnation, He decided that his identity during His first coming would be that of a servant.

Philippians 2:6-7

⁶...who though he existed in the form of God did not regard equality with God as something to be grasped, ⁷ but emptied himself by taking on the form of a slave, by looking like other men, and by sharing in human nature.

QUESTION 1

What word is used to describe both Christ Jesus' existence prior to His incarnation and his chosen lowly state during his time on earth?

Prior to his incarnation, Christ existed in the form of God. The word "form," as used here, denotes that expression of being that corresponds exactly to the reality. That is, Christ was fully God, and that was clearly evident to all in heaven. When He came into the world he laid aside that form (not His essential divine nature, but the outward expression of it), and took upon himself the form of a slave. The same word, with the same meaning, is used to describe his state on earth. He exchanged the form of God for the form of a servant. Jesus was truly a servant, and that was evident to all.

Read Phil. 2:1-11, and then answer the following questions:

QUESTION 2

What is the emphasis of this entire passage?

QUESTION 3

What specific admonition introduces the passage about Christ Jesus' humbling himself (v.5)?

When His disciples sought leadership positions and honor in His kingdom, Jesus contrasted the world's pattern of leadership with His own.

Mark 10:42-45

42 Jesus called them and said to them, "You know that those who are recognized as rulers of the Gentiles lord it over them, and those in high positions use their authority over them.

43 But it is not this way among you. Instead whoever wants to be great among you must be your servant,

44 and whoever wants to be first among you must be the slave of all.

45 For even the Son of Man did not come to be served but to serve, and to give his life as a ransom for many."

QUESTION 4

What prerequisite for leadership does Jesus set forth in these verses?

Shortly before His death Jesus taught His disciples a powerful lesson about what it means to be a servant leader by washing their feet. Please read John 13:1-16, and then answer the following questions.

QUESTION 5

How certain was Jesus about His identity? Where did He find His identity? What is the relationship between Jesus knowing His identity and the action He took to lower Himself to wash the disciples' feet (vv.3-4)?

QUESTION 6

Why do you think Peter resisted having his feet washed by Jesus?

QUESTION 7

How did Jesus persuade Peter to allow him to wash his feet (v.8)?

QUESTION 8

How does Jesus summarize the lesson He was seeking to teach through his humble act of service (vv.12-16)?

Topic 2: Combining Service with Leadership

Combining service with leadership is a challenge. How do we combine the two without diminishing either one? The Bible gives us the answer.

A key to understanding the biblical approach to combining leadership with service is to understand the terms used for servant in the Bible. *Doulos* is the most common Greek term used for servant in the NT. It's often translated slave or bondservant. It means "one who belongs to another." It views a servant in relationship to his master.

This is the term Paul used to describe Jesus in Philippians 2:7, where he says He took on Himself the form of a slave. Jesus chose to come into the world as a servant. As such, He had one ambition: to please His Master, the Heavenly Father. In John 4:34 He said, "My food is to do the will of the one who sent me and to complete his work." In John 5:19 He said, "I tell you the solemn truth, the Son can do nothing on his own initiative, but only what he sees the Father doing. For whatever the Father does, the Son does likewise." Everything He did was to obey and serve the Father.

This is also the term Jesus used in Matthew 10:24-25, when He said, "A disciple is not greater than his teacher, nor a slave greater than his master. It is enough for the disciple to become like his teacher, and the slave like his master...."

We Serve One Master and Seek to Please Him Only

Jesus calls us to be His servants. He is our Lord and Master. In Matt.6:24 Jesus said, "No one can serve two masters, for either he will hate the one and love the other, or he will be devoted to the one and despise the other. You cannot serve God and money."

In 2 Cor 5:9 Paul said, "…We make it our ambition to please him."

Just as Jesus came into the world as a servant of the Father, He has sent us into the world as His servants (John 20:21).

"Servant" Is Our Identity

It is clear from Scripture that we are to find our identity in being a servant, rather than in being a leader. As we serve, whether as a leader or in some other role, we must do so as servants of Christ, who have an obligation to please our Master.

> **A Servant Leader's Understanding of his/her Identity**
> I AM a servant, not merely one who DOES ACTS of service.

What is the difference between a leader who is truly a servant and one who merely does acts of service? A true servant leader finds his or her identity in being a servant, rather than in being a leader. It is a matter of heart attitude. Those who find their identity in being a leader may find it all too easy to begin doing acts of service simply to manipulate others and develop a mentality in which they expect others to serve them.

What does it mean to be a "*doulos*" – a true servant? It is my identity I live out of, not an activity that I do. It is who I am. It tells me that I belong to another.

Serving Is Our Task

The other key word for servant in the New Testament is "*diakonos*," from which we get the English word "deacon." It is defined as "one who serves others" and views a servant in relationship to his or her work.

In Matthew 23:11 Jesus declared, "the greatest among you will be your servant."

In Mark 10:44-45 He added, "And whoever wants to be first among you must be the slave of all. For even the Son of Man did not come to be served but to serve, and to give his life as a ransom for many."

In verse 44, the word translated slave is *doulos*, and in verse 45 the word translated "served" and "serve" is, in both cases, the verb form of *diakonos*.

In 1 Corinthians 3:5 Paul uses the term *diakonos* to refer to himself and Apollos:

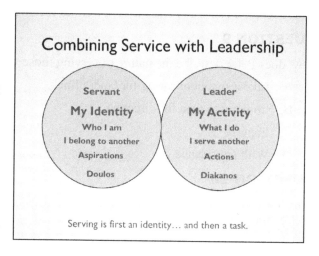

> ⁵ What is Apollos, really? Or what is Paul? Servants through whom you came to believe, and each of us in the ministry the Lord gave us.

Note that his emphasis in this verse is upon their differing ministries.

If *doulos* is my identity, then *diakonos* is my activity. If *doulos* is who I am, then *diakonos* is what I do. If *doulos* reminds me that I belong to another, *diakonos* reminds me that I am to serve others. *Doulos* centers on my aspirations, while *diakonos* centers on my actions.

Serving is first an identity and then a task.

How does this play itself out in daily life? I am first a servant (*doulos*) of Christ who serves (*diakonos*) others in various roles. I belong to the Master and serve only Him in whatever role He desires for me to have at the moment.

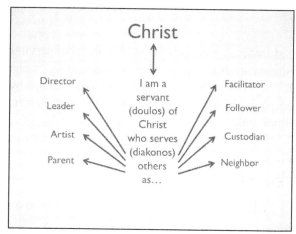

If your identity is as a leader, you are setting yourself up for an identity crisis, for at some point you will be asked to *not* lead. Then where will you be? The real test for leaders comes when you have to transition your leadership. But if your identity is as a servant, then when you are asked to not lead, you're okay because there is never unemployment for servants. You can serve on someone else's team, or you can lead a team. It doesn't matter, because your identity is as a servant.

Topic 3: Becoming a Servant Leader

Jesus became a servant leader by letting go of His existence in the form of God, emptying Himself and taking on the form of a slave. In like manner, if we would be servant leaders, we must be willing to let go of anything in our lives that is inconsistent with our identity as a servant of God.

The Apostle Peter struggled with this process but ended up with a clear understanding of what is involved in being a servant leader.

Please read 1 Peter 5:2-4 and then answer the following questions:

QUESTION 9

How does Peter describe the nature of serving those we lead? *(Select all that apply.)*

    A. Like a shepherd caring for God's flock

    B. Looking to God for direction

    C. Eagerly

    D. With confidence

QUESTION 10

What do you think "do not lord it over those entrusted to you" means? What are some examples of lording it over others?

QUESTION 11

In practical ways how does being a servant leader impact your ministry?

Good leadership is essential in all aspects of serving within the body of Christ. Whether the leadership position carries a large or small responsibility, it challenges our very identity and understanding of authority. Our style of leadership is often colored by the pattern of the world, which reflects attitudes that are frequently self-serving or authoritarian in nature. The leader often finds his or her identity in the position held. The biblical pattern of leadership is very different. The leader should find personal identity in Christ, allowing him or her the freedom to serve others without thought of protecting or defending the leadership position.

EXERCISE 1

Share with another person what you have learned about what it means to be a servant leader from this lesson.

Pray for one another.

Lesson 1 Answers to Questions

QUESTION 1: Form. Prior to His incarnation, Jesus existed in the form of God; during His incarnation he took upon Himself the form of a servant.

QUESTION 2: *Your answer should be similar to the following:*
The importance of humbling ourselves, following the example of Christ in His incarnation.

QUESTION 3: *Your answer should be similar to the following:*
You should have the same attitude toward one another that Christ Jesus had.

QUESTION 4: *Your answer should be similar to the following:*
Becoming a servant of other believers,

QUESTION 5: *Your answer should be similar to the following:*
Jesus was very certain about His identity. He found His identity in His relationship with His Father. The fact that His identity was rooted in His relationship with His Father freed Jesus to humble himself before His disciples.

QUESTION 6:
Your Answer

QUESTION 7: *Your answer should be similar to the following:*
He told him "If I do not wash you, you have no share with me."

QUESTION 8: *Your answer should be similar to the following:*
I am your Lord and Teacher yet washed your feet. In like manner, you should be willing to wash one another's feet. Follow my example, serving one another as I have served you, for you are not greater than me.

QUESTION 9
  A. Like a shepherd caring for God's flock
  B. Looking to God for direction
  C. Eagerly

QUESTION 10:
Your Answer

QUESTION 11:
Your Answer

Lesson 2: What are the Personal Qualities of a Servant leader?

"...set an example for the believers in your speech, conduct, love, faithfulness, and purity."
— 1 Tim 4:12

The Titanic was thought to be an unsinkable ship, but it was sent to a watery grave by a single iceberg. The part of the iceberg that sunk the Titanic was not visible but hidden beneath the waves of the North Atlantic. The personal life of a leader is like that unseen part of an iceberg, normally not visible to others, but wielding great influence over his or her ministry, for good or ill.

This lesson will give you the opportunity to reflect on some personal areas that are important to your role as a servant leader. Your leadership role puts you in a position where others will look to you not only for direction in the study of a course but also as an example to follow. Your devotion to God, your character, your manner of speaking, your vision for ministry, and how you manage your time will be communicated in words and actions as you spend time with them. We hope that you will be encouraged as to the good things God has been doing in your life and will want to press on to excel still more. Perhaps you will also become aware of areas that you feel need special attention.

Lesson Objectives

As a result of studying this lesson, you will:

- Be able to identify personal areas in the life of a servant leader that influence his role as a leader
- Be motivated to continue growing in each of these areas
- Respond by evaluating your personal life and making adjustments as needed

Lesson Outline

Topic 1: Devotion to God

Topic 2: Quality of Character

Topic 3: Manner of Speaking

Topic 4: Vision for Multiplying Disciples

Topic 5: Managing Time

> **Suggestion for Facilitators:** The topics in this lesson may best be studied as separate devotions at the beginning of several different study sessions. Practical exercises are included with each topic that would make excellent discussions for small groups. If you rush through these topics in just an academic way, the importance and intended impact for the students will most likely not be realized.

Topic 1: Devotion to God

As we think of living a life pleasing to God, nothing is more central than our devotion to Him. It touches the very root of our relationship with Him, and it is our motivation for why we do what we do. Being devoted to God brings to mind three descriptive words: love, commitment, and submission. So often we make the mistake of defining our devotion to Him in terms of the ministry we perform, not in terms of our heart relationship to Him. Our ministry should be an expression of a heart completely devoted to Him.

Exercise 1

Read Mark 12:28-34; 2 Corinthians 5:14; Romans 12:1-2; 1 Samuel 13:14; Psalm 139.

- Jesus teaches in Mark 12:30 that the greatest of all commandments is to love God with all our heart, soul, mind, and strength. Consider how loving God with each of these four parts of our being, deepens our devotion to Him.
- What does Paul say is the controlling motivation in his life (2 Corinthians 5:14)? As you consider Paul's life, why do you think he would come to this conclusion?
- Psalm 139 gives us a good look into the heart of David and his relationship with the Lord. List ways that David understood God's knowledge of him. What are David's responses? In practical ways, how does our devotion to God impact our teaching others?
- Allow time for personal reflection and prayer.

Topic 2: Quality of Character

Biblically, character is measured not only in terms of what we do but also by how we do what we do. As we evaluate the character of people, we need to consider their manner of life, not just the things they do and say. In the secular world, what a person is able to do often seems more important than issues of character. However, in choosing people to serve in the body of Christ, the quality of a man or woman's character should rise to the same level of importance as the person's gifting to serve.

Exercise 2

Read 1 Timothy 3:1-13; Titus 1:5-9; 2 Peter 1:5-9.

- From the Timothy and Titus passages make a list of the character qualities for elders and deacons. Are there any tasks included in the list?
- Why do you think Paul is giving so much emphasis to the character of these leaders?
- How does 2 Peter 1:5-9 describe the relationship of our character to our understanding of God's forgiveness for us? (See verse 9.)
- In practical ways, how does the quality of our character impact our teaching others?
- Choose one or more character qualities you would like to strengthen in your life. Share them with another person and pray together about these issues.

Topic 3: Manner of Speaking

The words we speak are often very revealing about the attitude of our heart and how we think about other people. With our words, we can build other people up or we can tear them down. We can speak words of encouragement or discouragement, words of forgiveness or pride or arrogance, words of honesty or dishonesty. Many more such contrasts could be given. Sometimes we wrongly think that speaking words of encouragement will make a person proud, but so often in Scripture we are exhorted to "encourage one another." Whether in our families or in our ministry, we need to give careful attention to the words we say and not neglect words of genuine encouragement.

Exercise 3

Read James 3:1-12; Ephesians 4:29; Colossians 4:6; Psalm 19:14.

- How is the nature of the tongue described in James 3?
- What does Paul say in Ephesians 4:29 should be the result of our words?
- What does Paul say in Colossians 4:6 should characterize our speech?
- What is David's prayer in Psalm 19:14 about the words he speaks?
- In practical ways, how does the manner of our speaking impact the teaching of others?
- Take time with one other person to speak words that encourage, that build up, and that are seasoned with grace. Would these words be pleasing in the sight of the Lord?
- Memorize Psalm 19:14.
- Pray for one another concerning your manner of speaking.

Topic 4: Vision for Multiplying Disciples

The vision that guides one in his or her ministry will greatly affect the outcomes of the work. So often pastors or other church workers serve with a vision that is limited to what they alone can accomplish. They serve as if the success of the ministry depends on them. The thought of equipping others with a shared vision is frequently ignored or given little intentional effort. In order to meet the needs of the church around the world, our vision of ministry must be characterized by a vision for multiplying disciples.

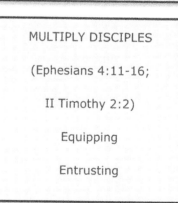

Exercise 4

Read Matthew 28:18-20, Ephesians 4:11-16, and 2 Timothy 2:2. Take time to meditate on these three passages, then answer the following questions:

- What commands did Jesus give to His disciples in Matthew 28:19-20? How are these related to one another?
- What does Paul say is the responsibility of the gifted leaders in Ephesians 4:11-12?
- What are the practical outcomes of equipping others to serve (Eph 4:12-13)?

- How does our commitment to making disciples impact the stability and growth of new believers and the church (Eph 4:14-16)?
- What instructions does Paul give Timothy about multiplying disciples in 2 Timothy 2:2?
- In practical ways, how does having a vision for multiplying disciples impact our teaching of others?
- How would you evaluate your commitment to making and multiplying disciples?
- Pray for one another, that God would enable each of us to be faithful to make disciples, and that multiplication would take place as those we disciple make disciples of others.

Topic 5: Managing Time

Each person is given the same amount of time to use each day, but there never seems to be enough time in a day to accomplish the things to be done. In thinking about this dilemma, it is good to be reminded that Jesus had the same amount of time available each day as we do, and He was able to accomplish the work given to Him by His Father. Scripture encourages us in Ephesians 5:15-16: "Therefore be very careful how you live—not as unwise but as wise, taking advantage of every opportunity, because the days are evil." So much of our frustration with lack of time is directly related to accepting responsibilities without evaluating the time needed to carry them out. The assuming of a new responsibility needs to be evaluated considering all present responsibilities and commitments. Your involvement as a student and as a facilitator brings added time commitments to what may already be a very full schedule.

Exercise 5

Read Luke 10:38-42, then answer the following questions:

- What did Jesus chide Martha for doing (v.41)?
- What was the "better part" that Jesus said Mary had chosen?
- What are the things that distract you from sitting at Jesus' feet and listening to Him?
- How can you rearrange your schedule to give priority to the most important things? As you do this, consider the time needed for personal devotions and Bible study, time with your family, ministry responsibilities, other work commitments, church commitments, recreation, and free time.
- Do you have a scheduled time for studying the BEE courses? How will you schedule the needed time for your preparation and facilitating of courses for your students? Do you consider this ministry a priority?
- Meditate on the following verses and record your observations in your Life Notebook: Psalm 90:12; Psalm 39:4-5; 2 Timothy 2:15.

> **Suggestion for Facilitators**
> Use the "Time in a Jar" illustration in Appendix 3 to impress upon your students the importance of giving priority to the more important things God would have them do.

Lesson 3: How Are Servant Leaders Developed?

*"Men are God's method.
The church is looking for better methods; God is looking for better men."*
— E. M. Bounds

The development of servant leaders is a very challenging task. It requires substantial effort on the part of both the training team and their trainees over an extended period of time. In addition, it requires a very different approach to training than most leaders have previously experienced. This lesson introduces this approach to training and gives an overview of the entire process that is required for the desired result to be achieved. The balance of this manual is composed of a more detailed step-by-step guide to implementing the training program.

Lesson Objectives

As a result of studying and applying this lesson, you will:

- Be able to describe the training method and process that is required for success in multiplying servant leaders
- Be able to explain why adopting this approach to training is so important
- Respond by committing yourself to do your best to complete all three phases of the training program

Lesson Outline

Topic 1: The Training Method: Facilitated, Interactive Learning

Topic 2: The Training Process: Three Phases of Development

Topic 1: The Training Method: Facilitated, Interactive Learning

Few can replicate a lecture, while many can facilitate interactive learning.

The most common form of teaching used in education throughout the world is the lecture method. The teacher or professor presents content through a lecture; the student listens, writes down what seems important, and then tries to remember what was taught. Generally, the teacher does not encourage questions or interaction except through the form of a written test or paper. The use of the lecture primarily focuses on the student gaining a certain level of knowledge about a subject.

> **Suggestion for Facilitators:**
>
> Use a T-chart to help your students think through the differences between lecturing and facilitating, and why those differences matter when it comes to training servant leaders.

A facilitator's approach to training is very different from a lecturer's. A facilitator engages his trainees in an interactive learning process through the use of questions and other learning activities. While a lecturer focuses on the transfer of knowledge to his listeners, a facilitator focuses on his trainee's understanding and application of principles. The use of the lecture, though important, takes on a lesser role, because the BEE course contains the primary content.

The facilitator does not repeat the content of the course through lecture, nor does he present all new material. Instead, he helps the students understand and apply material already studied, using questions and other learning tasks to facilitate learning. This approach to training makes it possible for more people to learn to train others and encourages a broader and better use of the course material.

Another important aspect of this form of training is that it is conducted within the context of a small group. This makes it possible for every trainee to ask questions and interact with both the facilitator and the other trainees. The facilitator will encourage this as he seeks to help the trainees better understand and apply the material.

You can expect some difficulties as you begin facilitating a new group using the interactive method, because this way of teaching may be new to your students. Your commitment to this way of instruction and patience with yourself and your students will determine how successful you will be in facilitating courses with your group.

Exercise 1

How would you describe the teaching methods used in your country? In your church? By you? If you have taken courses taught through interactive instruction, what were some of your responses to this way of teaching?

Topic 2: The Training Process: Three Phases of Development

As you work your way through the lessons in this manual, you will learn much about the process of developing servant leaders. At this point we want to gain an overview of the entire training process, which includes three phases of development: facilitating courses, training others, and mentoring for multiplication.

Phase 1: Facilitating Courses

You will first learn to facilitate the courses you have studied to a group of your own. Through your facilitation you are helping the students increase their biblical knowledge and understanding, grow in their development of godly character, and strengthen their ministry skills. The students should come to training events having already studied the assigned course material. This is very important and necessary to enable the facilitator to focus on what the students really understand and how they are applying what is understood. The facilitator accomplishes this through the use of good questions and other interactive forms of instruction. It is only as the students begin to express their thoughts about the course material that the facilitator can have reasonable certainty they are comprehending the important truths and concepts presented.

Phase 2: Training Others

The second phase of the training process is to learn how to train others to start their own groups and facilitate the same courses for others. You will learn the importance of modeling facilitation, and how to explain why you train the way you do. Then you will learn the importance of providing opportunities for your trainees to ask questions about this interactive way of learning. You also learn to let your trainees practice what they are learning about facilitating, either in small groups or before the entire class. You want your trainees to be able to say with confidence, "I can facilitate these courses also!"

An important aspect of your training ministry is to equip your trainees with a variety of ministry skills. As a facilitator, you are not only strengthening your trainees spiritually, but also developing them as leaders. Equipping them with a variety of ministry skills will increase their confidence as servant leaders and enable them to better help those they train develop as servant leaders. In addition, these ministry skills will make them much more effective in their larger ministry.

Phase 3: Mentoring for Multiplication

The third phase of the training process is to mentor your trainees through the process of establishing an indigenous multiplying training system. Regularly present to your trainees the vision of developing an ongoing training system to serve the biblical training needs of the church or churches in their areas of ministry. Each of your trainees will be facilitating a second-generation group of his or her own, facilitating the same courses you are facilitating to them. You will need to come alongside them as they seek to help their trainees do the same, multiplying the training to the third and fourth generations. Each trainee will need a lot of encouragement and counsel as he seeks to mentor others through the process of developing a multiplying training system.

Layering Learning

Developing servant leaders is a daunting challenge! Breaking the process down into manageable parts makes it much more doable. While this manual presents the process as involving three phases, it is important to note that all of these phases should be kept in view from the beginning to the end of the process. Accordingly, these three phases should also be viewed as responsibilities you will need to carry out simultaneously. Each responsibility should be carried out in light of the other two responsibilities to make the learning complete for your students.

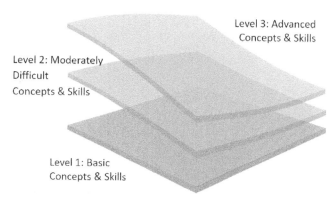

In view of this, it is recommended that you read this entire manual early in the training process, then go back through it more slowly, carefully studying it unit by unit as you move through each phase of the process. Units 2, 3, and 4 correspond to these three phases. You and your students should bring this manual you to every training event, layering learning as you are being trained and then as you train others.

Exercise 2

Read the three phases/responsibilities again.

Do you understand each one clearly? If not, what do you not understand?

Take time for each member in the group to explain in his own words the three phases/responsibilities. What do you think is meant by this statement? *Each responsibility should be carried out in light of the other two responsibilities to make the learning complete for your students.*

Unit 2: Facilitating Courses

Unit Introduction

The ability to effectively facilitate BEE courses is the foundational skillset upon which the entire process of multiplying servant leaders is built. This unit provides both the rationale for facilitation as a teaching method and a step-by-step guide to developing the skills required to be an effective facilitator. It is quite common for people who are used to being taught by the lecture method to resist facilitation at first, so it is critical that a facilitator be able to explain why facilitation is a more effective training method than lecture alone. It is also imperative that trainees experience a good model of facilitation, as the effectiveness of this training method becomes self-evident as it is experienced.

Unit Objectives

As a result of studying this unit, the BEE student will:

- Be able to teach interactively, using the BEE course workbooks, good questions, and creative learning activities
- Be able to write lesson plans
- Be committed to facilitating learning through interactive teaching
- Develop skill in leading a small group training session

Unit Outline

Lesson 4: Teaching Interactively

Lesson 5: Using the Course Workbook

Lesson 6: Using Questions to Facilitate Learning

Lesson 7: Using Creative Learning Activities

Lesson 8: Writing Lesson Plans

Lesson 9: Learning to Lead a Small Group Training Session

Lesson 4: Teaching Interactively

Learn to teach and train interactively…
you will follow in the steps of the greatest of all teachers—Jesus!

A foundational skill required if we are to multiply servant leaders for the church is the ability to teach interactively[1]. Few church leaders have been trained to teach in this way, and some even feel it is not really teaching. However, when we look closely at how Jesus taught and trained His disciples, we discover that interactive teaching is not only appropriate, but it is the preferred approach. Modern educational research has also demonstrated conclusively that interactive teaching is superior to traditional passive learner approaches to training.

Objectives

As a result of this lesson, you will

- Be able to explain why teaching interactively is the preferred method for facilitating the development of servant leaders
- Be committed to facilitating rather than lecturing the BEE courses
- Respond by identifying one or more barriers to teaching interactively in your culture and suggesting ways these barriers can be overcome

Outline

Topic 1: How Jesus Taught and Trained His Disciples

Topic 2: How the Apostle Paul Developed Servant leaders for the New Testament Church

Topic 3: How We Can Develop Servant leaders for the Church Today

Topic 1: How Jesus Taught and Trained His Disciples

In Lesson 3, we saw that Jesus used interactive teaching methods, especially as He trained His disciples. Let's look a bit more carefully now at how He taught and trained His disciples.

The ultimate example of interactive teaching is the incarnation of Christ. God did not merely preach to us from Heaven; He sent His only Son to dwell with us. As He came into the world, Jesus did not merely proclaim God's Word, He *was* the Word: God came in flesh to interact directly with us (Jn 1:1,14). The form in which Jesus came is also instructive: He did not come as a respected professor of theology, but as a humble servant (Phil 2:5-8). He taught not only by His words, but by His life. Thus, the incarnation may be seen as the definitive model for disciple-making.

Consider how Jesus approached those whom He chose to disciple. First, He invited them to follow Him (Mt 4:18-22; Mt 9:9; Jn 1:35-51). Then He selected some from among those who responded to His initial call to become more intimately involved with Him (Mk 3:14-15). There were some who wanted to join

---

[1] "Interactive," as used in this manual, refers to a teaching/learning process in which two or more individuals engage in two-way communication to facilitate learning, not to interaction with a computer.

His chosen band of disciples whom He turned away (Mk 5:18-19; Mt 8:18-22). He challenged those who would follow Him to count the cost of discipleship (Lk 14:25-35), but also spoke of the rewards of those who were willing to pay the price (Mt. 19:28-30).

Jesus spent much time with the twelve disciples whom He called to be apostles. From the time He chose them until the end of His earthly ministry, they were with Him day and night. When He spoke to the multitudes, they were with Him; when the multitudes went home, they were still with Him. During those private retreats Jesus explained everything to them (Mk 4:1-2,10-12,33-34). However, Jesus' private time with His disciples was not all about work. He invited them to come with Him to a quiet place and get some rest (Mk 6:31).

Jesus frequently engaged His disciples in dialog, making provocative statements that stimulated discussion among them, and asking penetrating questions that elicited heart-revealing responses (Mk 8:14-21, 27-29). He dealt decisively with relational issues among them, confronting wrong motives and challenging them to live a life of service and sacrifice (Mt 20:20-28).

Jesus led by example, asking nothing of His disciples that He was not willing to first do Himself (Jn 13:1-17). He taught them to pray by praying (Mt 6:9-13); He taught them to use the Scriptures by using the Scriptures; He taught them to minister to the marginalized and vulnerable by breaching social conventions to minister to Samaritans, women, children, publicans, and sinners.

From the very beginning of the discipling process, Jesus made it clear that it was His intention to involve His disciples in ministry (Mt 4:19). In the beginning, He delegated simple tasks to them, such as baptizing (Jn 4:2). His ultimate goal, however, was to be able to turn the ministry over to them in its entirety (Jn 20:21).

Jesus developed His disciples' ability to minister through a careful process of modeling, instruction, giving them opportunity to minister themselves, and then providing feedback and additional training (Mt 9:36-10:42; Mk 6:7-13, 30-32; Lk 10:17-24).

As Jesus' life and ministry took Him closer to the cross, He focused his time increasingly more on those He was training for leadership, seeking to prepare them for His death and resurrection, and the responsibility they would have to carry on His ministry after He was no longer with them. He also taught them about the Holy Spirit, whom He would give to them to enable them to carry on His ministry (Jn 11:53-54; Mt 20:17-19; Jn 14-16).

Following His resurrection, Jesus continued His interaction with His disciples, appearing to them on numerous occasions, imparting the Holy Spirit to them and giving them His final instructions. (Mt 28:16-20; Mk 16:15; Lk 24:45-48; Jn 20:19-29; Acts 1:8).

Exercise 1

Read and meditate on the Scriptures above, and then make a list of principles you see in Jesus' ministry that you desire to incorporate into your own ministry as you seek to make disciples.

Topic 2: How the Apostle Paul Developed Servant leaders for the New Testament Church

The Apostle Paul, following the example of Jesus, taught and trained interactively as well. After preaching the gospel, he entered into dialog with those who responded, teaching them from the Scriptures.

Even from early in his Christian life, he was making disciples as evidenced by the fact that it was his own disciples who helped him escape from those seeking to take his life in Damascus (Acts 9:23-25). He described the ministry of the leaders of the church as including "equipping the saints for the work of the ministry" (Eph 4:11) and selected key men to accompany him on his missionary journeys, training them as they travelled together (e.g., Timothy, Acts 16:1-5).

Late in his life, he charged both Timothy and Titus to train faithful men and women who would be able to train others also (2 Timothy 2:2; Titus 2:1-8).

Exercise 2

Compare 2 Timothy 2:2 with Titus 2:1-8, then answer the following questions:
- Which specific groups of people was Titus instructed to directly teach or train (Titus 2:2-3,6)?
- How was Titus to train these groups (vv.7-8)?
- What groups were to be trained by others (v.4)?
- Why do you suppose Paul specifically excluded these individuals from Titus' direct training ministry (cf 1 Timothy 5:2)?

Topic 3: How We Can Develop Servant Leaders Today

Following the example of Jesus and Paul, we can and must be intentional about developing servant leaders for the church today. The following lessons are designed to help you develop this critical ministry.

You can expect some resistance as you begin teaching and training others using the interactive teaching method, as this form of teaching may be new for people in your culture. It is important to explain why you are using this method. Sharing the Biblical material above will help you make the transition to interactive teaching and training, as people come to see that it is actually more biblical than many of the less effective methods that have come to be commonly used in the church.

Following are some other reasons for adopting this way of learning:

Interactive Teaching is a Better Way to Learn.

Research has shown that people learn more and are better able to apply what they learn when they are actively involved in the learning process (see accompanying diagram).

Interactive Teaching is Transferable

While only a few are able to effectively reproduce a lecture they have heard, almost anyone can learn to teach interactively.

One of the reasons for this is that while particular gifts are required to be an effective preacher or lecturer, a wide variety of gifts can be employed in interactive teaching.

Interactive Teaching is more Effective for Character Development

While we hope that when we preach people will apply the Word of God to their lives, most need help in actually doing so. Interactive teaching is an effective way to move people beyond mere knowledge of truth to the application of it in their lives.

Learn to teach interactively, and you will be well on your way to effectively multiplying servant leaders for the church.

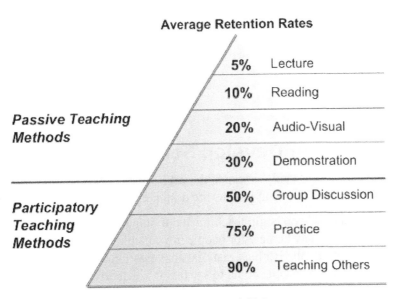

*Adapted from National Training Laboratories. Bethel, Maine

Exercise 3

What do you think will be barriers for you in facilitating courses to your students? If so, what are some ways to overcome them?

Lesson 5: The Course Workbook

The workbook is like a professor who has written out his lectures for the students.

The course workbook is the primary resource for the facilitator and student. The author of the workbook has communicated content through the grid of a particular design and structure. Understanding these two aspects, design and structure, enables the facilitator to better comprehend the flow of the course, resulting in more thoughtful and clearer teaching to the students.

Lesson Objectives

As a result of studying this lesson, you will:

- Be able to describe the design and structure of the course workbook
- Be convinced of the value of the course workbook as a transferable training tool
- Respond by using the course workbook as you study and facilitate BEE courses

> **Suggestion for Facilitators**
> The topics in this lesson would best be studied by having a course workbook available so the design and structure can be readily seen. Ideally, choose a course the students have already studied or will study next.

Lesson Outline

Topic 1: Design of the Course Workbook

Topic 2: Structure of the Course Workbook

Topic 1: Design of the Course Workbook

The course workbook was written with a particular design in mind. It is not that every workbook looks alike, but all are written in such a way as to accomplish certain common objectives. As a facilitator you should understand the design behind the course workbook. It will help you better understand the course material and enable you to facilitate the course toward its intended purposes with greater confidence. The following describes four major design factors incorporated when writing the course workbook:

Knowing, Being, Doing

The course workbook is designed not only to broaden the student's knowledge of a subject but also to address the needs of the whole person. The author writes the workbook keeping in mind three important concepts: knowing, being, and doing. *Knowing* refers to an intellectual and heart understanding of the content. *Being* refers to the inner response and character change, which results from understanding and application of truth learned. *Doing* refers to the practical outworking of what is learned in our daily lives and ministry. Throughout the workbook these three concepts are integrated into the written content and the variety of questions the students are asked to answer.

Self-Study

The course workbook is designed for self-study. The workbook provides written instructions to guide the student through the lessons. The workbook studies are written by authors who are able to bring the academic content about a subject to the written page. One could say the workbook is like a professor who has written out his lectures for the students. As a part of the written content, the author has included questions and exercises to enable the student to engage with the material in a meaningful way. Self-check tests and exams are provided to check the student's understanding of the most important issues and concepts.

Training Sessions

The course workbook is designed to be used in combination with training sessions led by a facilitator. These training sessions are designed to guide a small group of other students through the discussion of a BEE course. The training sessions will vary in time length, based on the circumstances of the students and the facilitator. The value of the time spent together in the training sessions is maximized when the students have completed the course work before coming. During the training sessions the facilitator will interact with the students, lesson by lesson, through all or part of a course workbook, helping them with understanding and application. The training session serves as the platform for the facilitator to fulfill the three responsibilities described in Lesson 3, each of which are reflected in the design and use of the course workbook.

Transferable Curriculum

The course workbook is designed to be transferable. This simply means that the workbook is written in such a way that a student who has studied the course and learned to facilitate it is able to use the workbook to teach the course to others. The workbook serves as both a student and teacher manual and should be provided to each succeeding generation of students. Remember, the workbook is like a professor. The students do not need to be the professor to teach others the course; they only need to be able to facilitate the same course they have already studied.

Topic 2: Structure of the Course Workbook

The structure of the course workbook will vary in small ways from course to course. This is mainly the result of the author's approach to the content to be covered and the desired outcomes for the student. Even though the structure is not exactly the same for every course, the general pattern is similar. This pattern will reflect three major structural parts: introductory structure, unit structure, and lesson structure.

Introductory Structure

The introductory material of the workbook is designed to give the student an overview of what can be expected in the study of the course and the requirements for successful completion. The introductory structure will be similar to the following:

Table of Contents: This provides an overview of units and lessons within the course.

Course Introduction: This describes the nature of the course and why the study of this subject is important to the life and ministry of the student.

Course Objectives: These bring into focus the desired outcomes as the student studies the course. The outcomes are expressed in terms of understanding the course content, character development, and personal application and ministry skills.

Course Organization: This gives students a review of the Table of Contents, which provides an overview of the units and lessons within the course.

Student Instructions: Not all courses include these, but when they are present, they describe what the students need to do as they study the course material in order to accomplish the desired results. This section will list the materials needed for the course, and preview assignments, special projects, self-check tests and exams that will be given during the course. It will also explain how the course is graded.

Unit Structure

Generally, the courses are divided into four units with three lessons each, but there will be some variations based on the how the content of a course has been structured. Unit structure will be like the following:

Unit Introduction: This briefly describes subjects to be discussed within the unit and why the study of this subject is important to the life and ministry of the student.

Unit Outline: This lists the lessons included in the unit.

Unit Objectives: These state the major desired outcomes for the student within the unit content. The outcomes are expressed in terms of understanding the course content, character development, and personal application and ministry skills.

Unit Exam: The unit exam tests the students' comprehension of the most important truths taught in the unit.

Lesson Structure

Even though there will be variations in the lesson structure within different courses, the general framework of each lesson will look similar to the following:

Lesson Introduction: This provides an overview of the content of the lesson. It helps the student anticipate the scope and sequence of the various topics to be covered before the study begins.

Lesson Objectives: These are provided to help the student understand the desired outcomes for the lesson. They are designed to help the student evaluate how well he has understood and applied the lesson.

Lesson Outline: This presents the different topics to be studied within a lesson.

Assignments: These assignments are in addition to the normal questions within a lesson and challenge the student to deepen his personal understanding and application of the lesson.

Topics: Topics identify the main subject areas of a lesson and provide the significant content for the student to study, understand, and apply. The number of topics will vary based on the needed content for the lesson.

Questions: Within the framework of each topic, a variety of questions will be asked to help the student interact with the content of the topic. Whenever students encounter a question in their workbook, they should stop and answer it. These answers should be marked or written down, either in the workbook itself or in a notebook (see the section on Life Notebook, below). At the conclusion of the lesson, students can then check their answers with those provided under the heading *Answers to Questions* at the end of the lesson. Questions and answers are numbered sequentially in each lesson to facilitate the checking of the student's work.

Life Notebook Questions: These are questions requiring more thought and written response than the general short-answer questions. Students are challenged more deeply in their understanding of the course content, encouraged to reflect on character and life-related issues, and stimulated in areas of practical ministry. The answers should be kept in a separate notebook, which should be brought to the sessions along with the course workbook. Answers are not provided for these questions. A significant portion of the session interaction will focus on the students' responses to these questions.

Exercises and Study Projects: Some courses have separate exercises and/or study projects. These study projects represent a larger study or activity designed to help the student internalize the concepts of the lesson. The projects provide students the opportunity to see how the concepts studied in the lesson can be applied, or worked out, in their own lives. Answers are not generally provided for projects, but each one will be evaluated and discussed during the session.

Self-check Test: At the end of each lesson a short test is provided to enable the students to review their understanding of the major concepts in the lesson.

Exercise 1

Compare the content of this lesson with an actual lesson in a BEE course. Are there areas that need clarifying?

Lesson 6: Using Questions to Facilitate Learning

"A prudent question is one-half of wisdom."
— *Francis Bacon*

Learning to ask good questions is fundamental to the role of the facilitator. Effective facilitators do not to make statements when they could ask questions, because they know that good questions can lead to meaningful discussions and greater understanding of the issues. The facilitator's knowledge of his students as well as his personal understanding and application of the material will greatly impact the quality of the questions asked. In addition, asking good questions will help the facilitator gain the confidence and respect of the group.

In this lesson we turn again to the example of Jesus, this time focusing on how he used questions. We will then consider in some detail several different types of questions every facilitator needs to know how to skillfully employ. These include introductory questions, inductive study questions, and follow-up questions. Finally, we will learn to evaluate questions to discern their effectiveness as facilitation tools.

Lesson Objective

To equip the facilitator to develop the skill of asking good questions

Lesson Outline

Topic 1: Jesus, Master Questioner

Topic 2: Introductory Questions

Topic 3: Inductive Study Questions

Topic 4: Follow-up Questions

Topic 5: Evaluating Questions

Topic 1: Jesus, Master Questioner

Jesus was very skillful at asking questions. Even though He knew His audience perfectly, He still used questions, both when preaching to the multitudes and when teaching His disciples. His questions challenged the thinking of those who wanted to learn, with a view to leading them to a better understanding of the truth. Of course, many of the religious leaders were not interested in the truth, and His questions confounded them. They even tried to trick Him with their own questions, but with no success.

> **Suggestion for Facilitators:** One of the most effective ways you can build the important skill of asking questions into your students is by encouraging them when they ask questions. If you respond to someone's good question by first saying, "That's a great question!" you will build them up and motivate the whole group to engage in discussion! (cf. Hebrews 10:24-25)

Like Jesus, we can and should use questions to facilitate learning for our students. Unlike Him, we do not know perfectly everything in the mind of our students, nor do we know all about their backgrounds and needs. Questions then become very valuable for us as a means of getting to know and understand our students. In addition, through the use of questions, our students' understanding of course concepts and issues can be revealed. In addition, questions are a way saying to our students, "I care about what you think," especially if we really listen to their answers!

As we spend time in meaningful dialog with our students, we will get to know them well. Periodically, asking questions of each person in the group to gather information helps the facilitator to better understand each one. Knowing the students' backgrounds, ages, work experience, family situations, special needs, and spiritual background will enable us to minister effectively to them. Understanding the dynamic and colorful picture of the group will help us develop appropriate questions that address the real needs of the students and lead them toward a deeper understanding and application of the truths of God's Word.

Exercise 1

Read the following passages, all of which contain examples of Jesus using questions. Following the example from Luke 7, complete the chart. listing the person or persons addressed, the question(s) asked and the impact of His questions for each of the other passages

Passage	Addressee	Question	Impact
Luke 7:40-50	Simon the Pharisee	Which of them (the two debtors whose debts were forgiven) will love him (the creditor) more?	Conviction (for Simon) and affirmation (for the sinful but repentant woman)
8:22-25			
9:18-20			
10:25-37			
13:10-17			

Topic 2: Introductory Questions

Introductory questions are used for three main purposes: 1) To encourage understanding of one another within a group, thus enabling the students to get to know each other better; 2) To help create a good atmosphere for discussion; and 3) To get discussion started, focusing the group members' attention on the topic of the lesson.

Sometimes called "ice-breakers," introductory questions should be open-ended and engaging, inviting those present to engage with one another and the topic of the lesson. Questions that make people feel uncomfortable should be avoided at the beginning of a lesson. Good introductory questions allow all group members to share from personal experience and encourage them to connect their answers to the topic to be discussed. They will help start the flow of discussion and encourage those who are a bit hesitant to speak more freely.

Examples of Introductory Questions

- Tell us about your family.
- Describe briefly how you came to Christ.
- What are some of the things you enjoy doing most?
- What is your least favorite task?
- What do you consider as one of your present greatest needs?
- Who would like to describe how you met your wife/husband?
- What is the most important thing on your heart right now?
- If you had only a day, week, or month to live, how would you spend your time?
- Do you carry an unfulfilled vision on your heart and mind? What is it?
- What are some ways you spend quality time with your children?
- What has encouraged you the most over the past week or month?

> NOTE: While Introductory Questions are asked first, it is often wise to prepare them after having prepared the rest of the lesson. Knowing where you want to end up is very helpful as you begin!

Exercise 2

Write down several examples of introductory questions that you think would encourage better understanding of one another and help to create a good atmosphere. Share the questions with the group.

Topic 3: Inductive Study Questions

The heart of the BEE approach to training is the Inductive Study Method. Skill in using this method in personal Bible study is developed in the Studying the Bible and Bible Study Methods courses. In this Lesson, we will learn how to lead a group through an inductive Bible study. This is done primarily through the use of inductive study questions. It is critical that the BEE facilitator become skilled at using questions to facilitate learning in the context of a BEE training session. This skill can also be effectively used in any small group Bible study setting.

There are three types of Inductive Study Questions: Observation, Interpretation, and Application. A study session should generally begin with observation questions, proceed through interpretation questions, and culminate with one or more application questions. These questions should naturally flow from one to the next, building upon the answers to previous questions. A short Bible study might cycle only through these three types of questions once, while a longer study might cycle back through some or all three types multiple times. For example, if a group is having difficulty properly interpreting a passage, the facilitator may ask additional observation questions to focus their attention on the important facts that need to be carefully considered in order for the correct interpretation to be discerned.

Observation Questions

Observation questions are asking, of the Scripture passage or other material being studied, "What does it say?" They are based on the *content* of the passage or course material studied. They are not questions focused on understanding the meaning, but questions designed to help the students gain a clearer picture of what the passage or material actually says. The answers to observation questions are *always* found in the passage or material studied. Generally, observation questions begin with one of these five key words: *who, what, when, where,* and *how*.

Examples of Observation Questions

- Who are the characters in this passage? What does the passage say about these individuals?
- What happened? List the facts set forth in the passage, without elaboration.
- When did this event happen?
- What is the distance between the two cities mentioned in the passage?
- Who is speaking in this passage? To whom is he speaking?
- What is the author's stated purpose in writing this passage?
- What is the specific circumstance or situation described in this passage?

Exercise 3

Find examples of observation questions in the course you are studying.

Write down two new examples of observation questions that you think would help you in understanding what the passage says.

Share your questions with the group. Have the group evaluate whether they are truly observation questions or not.

Interpretation Questions

Interpretation questions are asking the question, "What does it mean?" These questions are directed toward understanding the meaning of the passage or other material studied. Generally, they are prepared by choosing key words, ideas, or situations that are hard to understand or explain. Of course, answering interpretation questions correctly is very important. You do not want lots of different opinions that lead nowhere, but you are searching for the meaning intended by the author, first for his original audience, and only then for us today. When asking interpretation questions about passages in the Bible, there are four different places to discover the answer: (1) in the text, (2) in the context, (3) in other passages, and (4) other resource material such as a Bible dictionary, a commentary, a language dictionary, etc. The goal at this point in the process is to help your students understand the relationships between the key facts of the passage, its context, and other relevant information in such a way that the correct interpretation of the passage becomes evident.

At the same time, leading or limiting questions should be avoided. Leading questions, such as "You all agree with that, don't you?" stimulate no thought and stifle discussion. Limiting questions, such as "What are the three most important truths in this chapter?" stimulate little thought. The students know you have the right answer, so they will simply tell you what they think you expect of them. Open questions, such as "What do you think Jesus' words meant to his disciples?" stimulate discovery and understanding and promote discussion.

Examples of Interpretation Questions

- What does this word mean? What does it mean in the context? What does it mean as we use it today? How is this word used in other passages?
- What was the reason for this particular action or statement?
- What is the relationship between the two events in this passage?
- Why is this event or statement important? How does it affect the overall situation?
- What does this mean in the context it was written?
- How does this passage fit into the context of the whole book?
- Why do you think the writer is addressing this person or group of people?
- What does this imply about God's relationship to man, and man to God?
- How would you summarize the message, the truth, or the principle in this passage?
- Is there anything in this passage you do not understand?

Exercise 4

Find several examples of Interpretation Questions in the course you are studying.

Write down two new examples of interpretation questions that you think would help you correctly interpret the meaning of a passage.

Share your questions with the group and ask them to evaluate whether discussion of these questions would be likely to lead to a correct interpretation of the passage being studied.

Application Questions

Application questions move the students to the all-important third stage of learning, leading them to ask themselves, "What is my response to the truths we just studied?" These questions are aimed at helping the student make the Scriptures relevant to current concerns and problems in everyday living. Application questions should flow out of and directly relate to the correct answers to your interpretation questions. At the same time, they should be open questions, so as to stimulate maximum thought and discussion.

Use sensitivity and creativity when asking personal application questions so as not to embarrass any member. One suggestion would be to ask the whole group to write down their applications and then ask if some would like to share what they have written. To encourage the students to express their thoughts, the facilitator should answer the question first!

When evaluating an application question, ask:
- How relevant is the question today? Does the question lead to action?
- Is the question personal? (Note: sometimes it is best to let individuals answer sensitive or embarrassing questions privately.)

Of course, application questions take on real value only if we genuinely desire to apply them to our personal lives or the relevant situations or problems we face.

Examples of Application Questions
- What one truth did you learn from this passage that you will apply in a relationship with a non-Christian this week?
- How do you plan to practically apply the truth we learned today in your own life? Be specific!
- How will you practically apply what you have learned in your family?
- What did you learn that will help you in witnessing to non-Christians? How will you apply this?
- What did you learn today that will help you encourage your brothers and sisters in Christ? Think of one person and make a plan to encourage this person.
- Can any of you remember something that happened to you that demonstrates how this principle or truth works out in real life?
- Based on your understanding of this passage write out one commitment to God you intend to make in your attitude and/or behavior.

Exercise 5

Find one or more examples of application question in the course you are studying.

Write down two new examples of application questions that you think would encourage application.

Share the questions with the group. Evaluate the value of each question.

Topic 4: Follow-Up Questions

These questions often come spontaneously to your mind as you seek to encourage the students to go deeper into the issue being discussed. These might be called "wide-open" questions. They will follow a prepared question and add awesome value to it. These spontaneous questions will stimulate broader interaction among all the students and help make the discussion more alive. More important, they will give the students a greater understanding of the topic under discussion. Learn to use these well, under the guidance of the Holy Spirit.

Examples of Spontaneous Questions
- That's really interesting. Can you expand on that?
- David, what are your thoughts on this passage?
- Does anyone have something to add to what David said?
- Rebecca, can you give an example to help us understand what you mean?

- Does anyone else have an example?
- Paul, you answered with lots of conviction! Why is this so important to you?
- Would someone like to share a personal experience related to this issue?
- Is there anything else that would be important to mention on this subject?
- Are there any other passages that could help us understand this issue better?
- Does anyone else have something they would like to share?

Exercise 6

Write down a few new examples of spontaneous questions that you think would encourage a fuller discussion of an issue.

Share the questions with the group. Evaluate the value of each question.

Topic 5: Evaluating Questions

The number of questions that can be asked for any passage or course lesson is almost endless. However, some questions are better than others. The facilitator's task is to identify and then skillfully use only the best, most appropriate questions for the group. Use many different types of creative introductory questions, and you will continue developing a better understanding of your students.

Some questions are better for personal study than for group discussion. When preparing to facilitate a class, try to anticipate how various members will respond to each question you consider using. Can it be answered with one word (e.g. "yes" or "no")? If so, it is probably not a good discussion question. Will the students, with a little effort, be able to find or think of good answers, or will they be trying to guess what's in your mind? Is the question liable to stir up a controversy that could get out of hand? Discussing controversial matters can be valuable, if the group is mature enough to handle it wisely. However, it is best in the early stages of a group's development to minimize controversy whenever possible.

Select questions that best focus on the key issues and will lead the student to a better understanding and application of the material. Learn to use open and even wide-open questions that give opportunity for the students to express their own views, especially at the Application stage of the lesson.

Seek to maintain a good balance between observation, interpretation, and application questions. A general rule would be to have one third of the questions from each type. A discussion will normally progress from observation to interpretation to application. In a dynamic group situation, however, these steps will often be rearranged, and the emphasis will vary. The observation step should always serve as the foundation for interpretation and application.

Use follow-up questions liberally. You will find these to be some of your most valuable questions as you facilitate a course.

Exercise 7

Take a passage of Scripture that you have already studied and develop a series of questions that flow from one to the other, taking the students through all three steps of an Inductive Bible Study.

Project

After you have begun to recognize and practice using different kinds of questions, you can continue to grow in your question-asking skill in each course you study. Notice how questions are written in the course workbook, and ask, "What kind of question is this: Observation, Interpretation, or Application?" and "Would it make a good discussion question?"

In your personal life, practice asking questions of other people—especially open questions. Instead of asking your spouse or children the closed question, "Did you work hard today?" You could ask, "What kinds of things did you do today?"

> **Suggestion for Facilitators**: Make it a practice in every course you facilitate from this point on to draw attention to questions you have just asked (whether from the workbook or of your own making) and ask, "What kind of question is this?" This habit will encourage your students to continue to grow in in their skill of recognizing and being able to formulate good questions.

Lesson 6 Answers to Exercises
Exercise 1

Passage	Addressee	Question	Impact
Luke 7:40-50	Simon the Pharisee	Which of them the two debtors whose debts were forgiven) will love him (the creditor) more?	Conviction (for Simon) and affirmation (for the sinful but repentant woman)
8:22-25	the disciples	Where is your faith?	Their lack of faith challenged
9:18-20	the disciples	Who do the crowds say that I am? Who do you say that I am?	Caused the disciples to reflect on people's response to Jesus, and drew out Peter's confession of faith
10:25-37	an expert in the Law	What is written in the law? How do you understand it? Which of the three (the priest, the Levite, or the Samaritan) became a neighbor to the man who fell into the hands of robbers?	Conviction of the sin of self-righteousness
13:10-17	Jesus' critics	Don't you untie and water your animals on the Sabbath? Shouldn't this daughter of Abraham be released from Satanic bondage on the Sabbath?	Conviction of the sin of hypocrisy (critics) and rejoicing (the crowds)

Lesson 7: Using Creative Learning Activities

"It is the supreme art of the teacher to awaken joy in creative expression and knowledge."
— Albert Einstein

Often, when thinking of teaching we primarily think of the lecture. In the previous chapter, we stressed the importance of using questions to facilitate learning. In addition to the skill of asking questions, there are a number of other facilitation methods that significantly enhance learning. In this lesson, we will consider some creative ways to facilitate learning. These different ways of facilitating can become valuable tools as we seek to provide our students with the best learning experiences possible. Some will be new to you, but do not let that hinder you from using them. Most are quite easy to learn, and wise use of a variety of facilitation methods will make you, and your students, much more interesting and effective facilitators.

Lesson Objectives

As a result of this lesson, participants will:

- Be able to list several creative facilitation methods and explain how they enhance learning
- Be motivated to give appropriate expression to the creativity God, the Creator, placed within them
- Be equipped to glorify God by skillfully using creative learning activities as they facilitate

Lesson Outline

Topic 1: Creative Facilitating

Topic 2: Team Facilitating

Topic 3: Student Involvement

Topic 4: Short Lectures

Topic 5: Guidelines for Effective use of Creative Learning Activities

Topic 1: Creative Facilitating

Using creativity in the facilitating of the BEE courses can greatly enhance the learning experience for the students and provide variety for both students and facilitator. For the most part you are limited only by your own imagination. Once you have set the example and thus freed your students to facilitate in creative ways, you will also benefit from their creativity. Here are a few ideas that will serve you well as you learn to incorporate creative learning activities into your facilitating.

Divide a Larger Group into Smaller Groups

The primary value of this method is to enable greater interaction among a greater number of people. Often within the larger group many do not feel free to share their thoughts. For example: You have a group with fifteen people, and you would like them to discuss a particular question. Break the group into three groups of five, or five groups of three. Ask them to interact on the question for a specific period of time, say ten minutes, then have one person from each group share with the whole group some of the main thoughts their small group discussed.

One-to-one Interaction

Ask a question and instruct your students to discuss it with the person seated next to or across from them. This serves the purpose of helping more timid students communicate freely their thoughts, which they may not do in the larger group. Afterward you can give the opportunity for some to share with the larger group.

Visual Aids

Someone has said, "A picture is worth a thousand words." The use of visual aids will often better explain a point than words alone, and the student will most likely not forget it! There is no limit to what you can use. It could be maps, pictures, drawings, objects from nature, small familiar objects, food, an action performed, and many, many other possibilities. Give opportunity for the students to think creatively with this one...they are full of unexpressed ideas!

Illustrations

Use characters from the Bible, events from history, current happenings, personal stories, things easily identified from work, school, family, etc. We often see Jesus using illustrations from all walks of life to teach a specific truth. Again, draw on the creative resources of your students!

Role-play

Have the students act out a story or truth you want them to remember. Give them freedom to develop the role-play as they would like. You will be amazed at what they create, and you will learn a lot about their personalities and gifting. The role-play not only brings to life the truths studied, but also deepens the relationships among the students.

Guest Teacher

Involve someone from outside the class who could give a special short teaching on a subject you are covering in a course. Make sure it is done in such a way that the students can ask questions and the main points in the course are being addressed. Make sure you know this person well, and that they can be trusted to use the opportunity in the right way. Set a time limit for this activity, and make sure to communicate to the guest teacher the importance of keeping his presentation within the allotted time.

Exercise 1

What creative facilitation methods have you observed your facilitators use? Which were most meaningful to you? Are there any that you felt were not helpful in the learning process?

Topic 2: Team Facilitating

Two are better than one because they have a good return for their work!

(Ecclesiastes 4:9)

Team facilitating is when two qualified persons agree to share the responsibility of facilitating a group. Each person needs to have an honest commitment to work together and to deal with problems that may arise between the two. The group can easily see how you relate to each other. If you work well together, there will be more respect from the group, and you will experience more joy in your task. If there is a leadership struggle, the group will quickly understand this, and they will gradually lose respect for your leadership.

Benefits of Team Facilitation

- Mutual encouragement
- Builds your relationship with one another
- Enables you to prepare and pray for students together
- Share the responsibility of leading the session
- Can alternate taking the primary role in leading the session
- Share administrative responsibilities
- Makes it possible for the session to go on if one facilitator becomes ill or is otherwise hindered from facilitating
- When one is leading, the other can be thinking about other helpful ways to contribute
- When one encounters difficulties while facilitating the other can assist him
- More opportunity to spend personal time with group members...meet more needs
- Large group can be broken into two smaller groups with each leading one group
- Evaluation of the session has broader input

Exercise 2

Discuss the concept and value of team facilitating. What are some of the challenges inherent in team facilitating? How might these be addressed?

Topic 3: Student Involvement

As a facilitator, one of your responsibilities is to train your students to be able to do what you do...to be a good facilitator! As you observe and get to know the students, give selected ones the opportunity to team facilitate with you for part or all of a lesson to the whole group[2].

Make clear what you want the student to do, what material (s)he is to cover, and give him or her time to prepare, at least a week's notice. If this is the student's first time to do this, plan to help with the preparation. But do not do all the preparation for the student! You want the facilitating plan to be theirs, not yours...so allow space for his creativity.

Tell the student you will be evaluating him or her. Your manner in evaluation is critical for you and the student. Give strong encouragement for effective facilitation and gently provide the counsel needed to help strengthen weak areas. You want to be a source of encouragement, not of discouragement. And you want the student to want to do it again!

Exercise 3

Discuss the concept and the learning value for the student who is involved in practice facilitating, as well as for the other students. At what point in the training process should you begin involving students in this way? What problems can arise if you start too soon? Too late?

Topic 4: Short Lecture

The session should not turn into a lecture!

The primary way of facilitating the session is through interactive learning. However, there are certain points in the lesson where short lectures can and should be used. Often (though not always), it is good to give a short lecture at or near the beginning of a lesson to introduce the subject or place it in context. Most creative learning activities will also be most effective if a short summary lecture is given immediately afterwards. Discussions often need to be brought to a fitting conclusion by means of a short lecture.

One habit pattern that should be avoided is failing to manage time well, and then trying to cover the parts of a lesson you didn't get to by means of lecture as time runs out. The last portion of a training event is often the most important, and it is critical that facilitators manage their time in such a way as to make it possible to end the class in the most effective way possible. Usually that requires giving the students opportunity to respond to the truths learned, rather than trying to cram a bit more knowledge into their heads by means of a lecture.

You may be a very gifted lecturer, and as a result want to teach in this manner more than using questions. It is critical that you remember that the goal of BEE training is not just to transmit knowledge, or even to inspire. It is to multiply trainers. If you spend most of your time lecturing, most of your students will not be able to replicate what you have done, as they don't have the same gift you have, and as a result multiplication will not take place. Use your gift, but don't over-use it, and be sure to facilitate in such a way that everyone is equipped to use his or her gifts to minister.

---

[2] Be careful not to give responsibility for too much of a lesson to a student who has not been adequately trained. If he fails to effectively facilitate the section he is given, you will want to have time to go over that section later, so that the learning for the whole class is not hindered.

Exercise 4

Discuss: What qualifies as a "short" lecture? How can a facilitator keep his lectures short?

Topic 5: Guidelines for Effective Use of Creative Learning Activities

While creative learning activities can enhance learning, they may also hinder learning. Because many of new BEE students have had little or no exposure to creative learning methods, and they have been trained to believe that real teaching only takes place through lecture, it is important that a facilitator assess the readiness of his students to accept unfamiliar ways of learning. It might be wise to begin by using a more traditional teaching approach, and gradually introduce facilitated learning. This should be accompanied by thorough instruction in why facilitation is the preferred method for training and multiplying leaders (see lesson 4).

Another issue that often arises as students are beginning to learn to facilitate is that creative learning activities are allowed to take up too much of the available time. It is very easy to underestimate the time needed for creative activities. If time is not managed well, an activity such as a skit can take up all the time allotted for a topic, and there is no time left for the summary of the lesson that is often critical to clarifying the point of the activity

Lesson 8: Writing Lesson Plans

"Success depends upon previous preparation, and without such preparation there is sure to be failure."
— Confucius

The facilitator's preparation for each lesson is central to how well he or she will be able to lead the students to accomplish successfully the objectives of a course. Different facilitators prepare in different ways, but all the best facilitators write out lesson plans for each lesson they plan to facilitate. In this lesson, you will learn why lesson planning is important and then be led through a step-by-step process of writing a lesson plan.

Lesson Objectives

As a result of this lesson, you will:

- be able to list and explain the steps to writing a lesson plan
- be motivated to write out lesson plans for all lessons you facilitate
- respond by writing a lesson plan for the lesson you will practice facilitate

Lesson Outline

Topic 1: Why is Lesson Planning Important?

Topic 2: An Overview of a Good Lesson Plan

Topic 3: A Step-by-Step Guide to Writing a Targeted Lesson Plan

Topic 1: Why is Lesson Planning Important?

The time available for training servant leaders is always limited. In order to make the most of the time we have with our students, we must carefully plan how we will use that time.

Well prepared lesson plans allow for varying conditions while still focusing on what is truly important in each lesson. All the information in a given lesson is important, but not everything is equally important. Knowing each lesson's most important ideas helps us choose what to cover. This is especially important if the time allotted for the lesson is unexpectedly cut short.

Students will only remember and take away a limited amount of information, so the facilitator must choose carefully what to emphasize. The students will be able to apply only what they remember. If there are too many areas of focus, the students may be overwhelmed and thus remember very little from the lesson. If the facilitator fails to focus adequately on the vital areas, applications will be missing as well.

Keep in mind that in the BEE system of training, the course is the professor. Students have the course material, with all the content of the course, so they don't need the facilitator to cover everything. It is not the job of a facilitator to re-teach all the material. Students are responsible to study all the material for a given class before coming. Covering all the material again in class does not honor the students' work and may even be demotivating.

Student leaders may have difficulty seeing the big picture of each of the courses and lessons unless they are mentored to develop this skill. The clearer our lesson plans are, the easier it will be for student leaders to learn to plan and lead strategically as well.

Learning and practicing the skill of forming targeted lesson plans will help us and our students use time wisely and become more effective leaders and multipliers.

Exercise 1

Reflect on the way you have prepared for leading a Bible study in the past. Compare the way you prepare with the way others in the class do and discuss the strengths and weaknesses of the various approaches.

Topic 2: An Overview of a Good Lesson Plan

What does a lesson plan look like? First of all, it is a *written* plan that is based on the material from the lesson. A plan that exists only in the mind of the facilitator is not adequate to keep a training session on target. On the other hand, it should not be an extremely detailed document that spells out everything that will be said and done during a training session.

Preparing to facilitate a lesson is quite different from preparing to preach or give a lecture. When preparing a sermon or lecture, the speaker asks himself, "What am I going to *say*?" When preparing to facilitate, the facilitator asks himself, "What are *my students* going to *do*?"

A good lesson plan contains four elements:

- A Key Concept Statement that summarizes the central truth of the lesson
- Lesson Objectives (what you want your students to know, be, and do as a result of the lesson)
- An Outline of the Lesson itself (what you and your students will say and do)
- Time estimates for each part of the lesson (which, added together, comfortably fit within the time allotted for the lesson).

> **Suggestion for facilitators:** As you facilitate this section of the lesson, it may be helpful to sketch a tree on the white board, drawing and labeling each part as you explain how it represents an aspect of a good lesson plan.

A good lesson plan may be compared to a tree:

Your preparation (prayer, study, writing the lesson plan) is represented by the root system of the tree. No one sees that part of a tree, but it is critical to the health of the tree. In like manner, the depth and quality of your preparation will make a great difference in the effectiveness of your facilitation.

The key concept, or central truth that you will be teaching through this lesson, is like the trunk of the tree. The main branches of the tree represent the Lesson Objectives, while the smaller branches and leaves of the tree represent the questions you will ask and the learning activities through which you will facilitate learning.

Finally, the fruit of the tree represents the application portion of the lesson.

Just as every part of a tree connects in some way to the trunk, in your lesson, everything—the objectives, the questions, the activities, and the application—should relate in some way to the key concept.

Topic 3: A Step-by-step Guide to Writing a Targeted Lesson Plan

Effective facilitation helps focus the energy, attention, and work the students have already done on the most critical concepts in each lesson, rather than re-teaching everything. This reminds students that the course, not the facilitator, is the professor and that it will be the tool that equips them to train the next generation.

Following these steps for lesson preparation will help aim students at the most important concepts for each lesson. Strategic and prayerful preparation helps deepen students' understanding, so that they will remember and apply what is most important in each lesson. This leads to life-changing impact.

1. Pray

Training others to be servant leaders is a spiritual ministry and cannot be effectively done without the enabling power of the Holy Spirit.

As you begin your lesson planning process, commit your time to the Lord in prayer, asking Him to give you insights into His Word, understanding of your students, and wisdom as you select learning activities. In addition, ask Him to give you just the right words as you prepare your questions and short lectures.

2. See the Whole Course (the Big Picture)

Review the contents of the whole course to see where this lesson fits.

Read the objectives for the lesson you are preparing to facilitate, and then scan the whole lesson to see how the objectives are developed.

3. Work Carefully Through the Lesson

Study or review the entire lesson, writing out your answers to all the questions and completing all the exercises, if you have not previously done so.

Ask God to use the course and the Scriptures it references to impact your own life or reflect on how it has already done so. Ask yourself, "Why is this lesson important?"

As you study or review the lesson, highlight key areas, verses, and questions, and record any ideas for facilitation that come to mind.

4. Choose Your Strategic Focus

Write out a key concept statement that expresses the main idea you will focus on in your lesson.

Considering the course objectives, the content of the lesson, and the needs of your students, choose or write out at least one objective in each of three categories:

- Knowing (what you want your students to know or understand as a result of your facilitation of this lesson)
- Being (what character qualities you want to see developed in your students through this lesson)

- Doing (the action steps you want to see your students take as they apply this lesson to their personal lives and ministries)

NOTE: It is helpful to write your objectives in the following form:

As a result of this lesson, my students will:

1. Be able to (explain, describe, etc.) (the truths you want them to know).
2. Be (motivated, encouraged, convicted, etc.) to develop in (a character quality)
3. Respond by (describe the action steps you want them to take)

Choose and list 6-8 of the most important concepts you will target as you facilitate the lesson. If possible, narrow this list to the 3-4 most critical areas for the "main ideas" circle of the Target. These should all relate in some way to the key concept.

5. Form Plans to Focus

Choose or write questions and exercises from the lesson that will help your students explore the important areas. Consider how much time students will need for discussion and discovery.

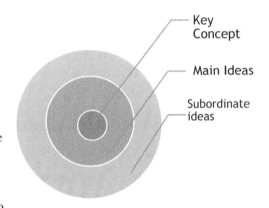

Carefully plan how you will engage the students in direct inductive study of the Scriptures. Review Lesson 6 and be sure you have a good balance of observation, interpretation, and application questions.

Choose one or more creative learning activities for inclusion in the lesson. Review Lesson 7 for ideas. Try to evaluate if what you have planned will be worth the time it will take, both when planning and in class. You might consider having a "menu" of different activities you could use, giving you flexibility to adjust to unforeseen circumstances.

Plan parts of lessons for students to practice facilitating, if they are at the point where that is appropriate.

Consider ways to cast vision and mentor for multiplication, i.e.: when using creative methods, ask students, "What did I just do? Why do you think we did this? How can you do this with your students?"

6. Summarize and Lead to Application

Summarize and restate the main concepts (target areas) for students to remember.

Write or choose two to three application questions you will use to guide students to apply the lesson. It will be helpful to review your knowing, being, and doing objectives as you prepare this part of the lesson plan.

7. Prepare Your Introduction and Conclusion

It is often helpful to wait to prepare your introduction to the lesson until after you have completed the main body of the lesson.

Prepare a short conclusion to encourage students. Plan to pray together, asking God for His continued work of transformation and thanking Him for all He has done.

Exercise 2

Read the sample lesson plan in Appendix 5

As your facilitator directs, prepare a lesson plan on the same lesson as other students, and compare your approaches and ideas.

Prepare your own lesson plan for a practice facilitation lesson and submit it to your facilitator for review prior to facilitating that lesson.

Lesson 9: Learning to Lead a Small Group Training Session

"The well-run group is not a battlefield of egos."
— Laozi

This Chinese proverb, written around 600 BC, describes in an insightful way what a small group should *not* be like! Judging from the date of this proverb, it seems that small groups have been around for a very long time.

Small groups are used in almost every area of society—the family, the work place, team sports, in schools, and the church—to build relationships and accomplish certain goals. As mentioned in an earlier lesson, Jesus used the dynamics of the small group to prepare the twelve disciples for their future mission of carrying out the Great Commission.

The small group is the primary context used by the facilitators to accomplish the three responsibilities they have toward their students. The BEE courses are best facilitated to a small group, and both the training of facilitators and mentoring for multiplication require small groups. In this lesson, we will consider the makeup of the ideal small group for the BEE training program, look at several principles for leading a small group, and discuss how to manage common problems that often arise. The lesson will conclude with some guidelines to help evaluate the leading and interaction of small group discussions.

Lesson Objectives

As a result of this lesson, you will:

- Be able to describe the ideal small group for BEE training, and explain how to lead effective small-group training sessions
- Be challenged to develop a passion for training servant leaders in a small group setting
- Respond by making a commitment to develop the skills needed to do effective training in a small group setting

Lesson Outline

Topic 1: Describing the Small Group

Topic 2: Leading a Small Group

Topic 3: Managing Common Problem Areas

Topic 4: Evaluating the Small Group

Topic 1: Describing the Small Group

As mentioned above, the small group is the primary context for facilitators to fulfill their role of accomplishing their three major responsibilities. The small group is led by one or more facilitators, who are responsible to give the needed leadership for the success of the group.

The small group learning sessions are *not* to be lectures where the facilitator talks most of the time, nor are they to be dialogues between only a few members in the group, while everyone else listens. Rather, they are to be characterized by active participation by all members of the group. **How large should a small group be?** An ideal number in a group for quality learning and good group dynamics is between six and eight persons. Whenever a larger number of students is involved, the large group can be divided into smaller groups. For example: If 15–20 persons are in the large group, three smaller groups of 5–7 persons each can be formed. Keeping the groups small will encourage greater interaction and learning by all.

The seating arrangement is also very important. Using the example above, have each group sit around a small table so they can see each other and the facilitator. This enables each person to speak directly to the others in the group. Sitting in rows only allows them to speak to the facilitator, and to the backs of other people's heads!

The contributions made to the lives of the student involved in a well-led small group can be life changing. A well-led small group:

- Encourages participation from everyone
- Builds relationships through the sharing of personal feelings, beliefs, and needs
- Stimulates the sharing of new ideas and convictions
- Develops leadership potential and abilities through active involvement
- Helps each person develop his own conclusions and convictions
- Encourages honesty and accountability about real life issues

Topic 2: Leading a Small Group

Permit the group to work! Facilitators should not regularly answer their own questions, express their own opinions, or make other contributions that they can elicit from the group.

Respect the value of each individual. Each person has his own thoughts and ideas. A good facilitator will want to know what each person thinks, not what *he* thinks the person should think!

Rephrase questions if needed. If someone or the whole group has difficulty answering a question, it is possible the question needs to be rephrased in a more understandable way.

Allow time for students to answer the questions. Ask the question, and then allow a reasonable amount of time for the group to think about the question. Do not hesitate to rephrase the question if there seems to be doubt about the meaning. If no one answers, you could call on someone whom you feel could give a response. Affirm the responses.

Encourage good discussion. Be ready to comment on answers, show approval, and ask other questions to stimulate discussion, understanding, and application. Allow good discussion to flow freely among the group members but take care to keep track of time so as to cover the desired content.

Take advantage of controversy. Differences of opinion can stimulate interest and thought by all members of the group. The aim of the leader is to guide rather than stifle the discussion. When individuals differ, encourage a resolution on the basis of the passage being studied. If the passage is not specific, several courses of action can be taken:

- Other passages of Scripture known to the group may provide the answer.
- Further study between sessions may lead to a clearer understanding.
- The disagreement may be irresolvable. If this is the situation each person should be encouraged to accept one another's difference in viewpoint even though not agreeing with the viewpoint. Make sure there is a clear understanding of each person's viewpoint.

Review periodically. At points where natural breaks occur ask summary questions that encourage the group to think through the previous progression and make clear the main ideas. This is also a good time for the leader to ask the members if they have any questions before going on to a new topic.

Emphasize the positive. No group member, under any circumstance, should be told bluntly that his answer is wrong! If a portion of an answer can be accepted and commented upon, it should be. Here are some possible comments you can make:

- "That certainly is a position commonly held today. Is there any real basis for it in the text?"
- "That is an interesting point. I imagine there would be varied opinions within the group. Does anyone else care to express his thoughts about this matter?"

Wrong theology should not be approved, but the way in which wrong answers are handled will encourage or discourage future group responses. Make sure that the member's answers to the leader's questions are clear. Good questions about his answer can help to clarify meaning.

Consider this: Raise the truth to the same level as any untruth that is being stated. Allow the Holy Spirit to lead that person to a right understanding of the truth being taught.

Wisely challenge superficial answers. Sometimes statements are made, and words used that are almost without meaning in today's world. Encourage the person to rephrase what is said into more contemporary language and to define terms that would lead to a better understanding of what was said. Here are some possible challenges:

- "How would you explain that word or term in your own words...or to a child?"
- "How would explain that idea to someone from another culture or who is illiterate?"
- "Could you give an illustration of what you mean?"

Occasionally use background information. This can be very helpful in stimulating a discussion, but it should be kept brief.

Larger groups. If the group is larger than eight, use questions that students can discuss among themselves in smaller groups of four or five persons. Later, have them share the results of their discussion in the larger group.

Topic 3: Managing Common Problem Areas

New or shy group members. Encourage participation with simple questions involving the expression of opinion or choice. Ask the student to read the passage being discussed. Break the group into pairs and ask a question they can discuss together. The new or shy person will feel freer to share their thoughts in this context. Be appreciative of every contribution.

Too talkative. Gently restrain by addressing questions to the others by name. It may be good to talk with the student after the study about this problem.

Little knowledge. Ask observation questions related to facts from the text until students are confident enough to give their own opinions and impressions.

Talks about unrelated subjects. Make clear the purpose of the study. Encourage students to talk about related subjects of genuine concern after the study. Example:

> "What you have mentioned could make for an interesting topic for discussion. Let's talk about that after our study. Okay?"

Irrelevant contributions. Ask "Where in the text did you find that?" Or in some other way urge the student to get ideas from the passage or study material.

Always looks for problems. Some students like to focus on problems that are have little relevance to the main point of the lesson. These issues should be deferred, so the class can concentrate on the positive teaching that can be understood. Sometimes these problems are answered later in the discussion; if not, they should be discussed separately from the group. Here are some examples of how to do this:

> "The problem that you have mentioned is a good one. As we continue to study the passage, I think the answer will be made clear to us."

> "The problem that you have mentioned is a difficult one which cannot be answered in our particular study today. Let's discuss this issue after class."

Likes to show off knowledge. When a student frequently digresses from the text by quoting other parts of Scripture, show him or her the value of keeping to the passage. Be appreciative when the contribution is appropriate to the discussion and is helpful in clarifying a difficulty. Example:

> "We may need to look at that passage later, but for the present, let's see if we can continue to discover additional insights in the passage before us."

Periods of silence. This may mean the members are giving good thought to the question asked. To have meaningful discussion, there must be time to think. However, you should try to discern the difference between fruitful silence and empty, confused silence. Rephrasing the question may be necessary. However, remember not to answer your own questions!

Topic 4: Evaluating the Small Group

As we are learning to lead a group, we should be periodically evaluating how we are doing. Taking the time for evaluation will be of benefit for both the leader and the group. The best time is shortly after a group session, while all is still fresh in your mind. Actually, involving the whole group in doing the evaluation could be very constructive for everyone. This would help each group member better understand the value of good group dynamics. Group evaluations should be carefully guided so as to ensure they are constructive in nature. When evaluating a respected leader's facilitation, the group may be inclined to give only positive feedback. When evaluating each other, group members may go to the other extreme, giving too much negative feedback. These problems can be solved either by having the group provide anonymous, written evaluations, or by modeling constructive oral evaluation.

Written evaluations should be simple in nature, perhaps including only two questions, such as:

1. What was particularly helpful to you in this session?
2. What is one suggestion you have for improvement?

An oral evaluation session will prove most constructive when it follows a "sandwich" formula, as follows:

1. Solicit and give positive feedback. Ask your students what they liked about the session, then add your own affirming comments.
2. Give constructive suggestions for improvement. Again, ask your students for their suggestions, then add your own.
3. Give more positive feedback.

An evaluation should be used only periodically, not after every session. The evaluation is to serve as an encourager, corrector, and strengthener of the small group. Learning to lead a group takes time, so be patient. The more experience you gain, the more the skills involved in leading a small group will become natural for you.

Below are a number of evaluation questions that can help evaluate the group discussion, your leading of the group, and the spiritual benefits to the students. Most of these questions can be answered with "yes" or "no." They are designed to raise the issues and open the door, if desired or needed, for discussion about a particular issue that needs to be addressed.

Group Discussion

- Was everyone present and on time?
- Did the discussion flow well?
- Was all the important material covered?
- Was everyone involved in the discussion?
- Were there any significant problems raised by the students?
- Was there a good atmosphere?

Group Leader

- Were you well prepared? Did you need more time for study? How much?
- Which questions stimulated the best discussion? Why?
- Which questions stimulated the least discussion? Why?
- Did you answer your own questions?
- Did you lecture or carry on extended conversations with one or several members?
- Were you encouraging, enthusiastic, and confident?
- Did you reflect a learner's attitude and vulnerability?
- Did you force your ideas on the group?
- Did you follow your lesson plan?
- Did you give good opportunity for practical application of content discussed?
- Did you conclude the discussion with a clear summary?
- Did you begin and end the meeting as scheduled?
- Did you involve others with group arrangements, materials, facilitating?

Spiritual Benefits
- Are the students growing in knowledge and understanding?
- Are attitudes and actions being changed?
- Are the students growing spiritually?
- Is there an increasing commitment to one another?
- Is there a freedom to share from one's personal life?
- Is there a desire to share with others what is learned?

Exercise 1

Review and discuss the above content. Do you have anything you do not understand?

Break the group, if necessary, into smaller groups of five or six people.
- Choose a leader for each group.
- Using Introductory Questions of your choice, have the leader guide a discussion for about fifteen minutes.
- Have each group evaluate its leader and the quality of the discussion for five minutes.
- Choose another leader for each group.
- Choose one or two Life Notebook questions from one of the lessons in the course you are currently studying, then have the leader guide a discussion for fifteen minutes.
- Have each group evaluate its leader and the quality of the discussion for five minutes.
- Evaluate and summarize the time in the larger group; then give opportunity for any appropriate questions.

Unit Three: Training Others

Unit Introduction

Once the BEE student has mastered the ability to facilitate BEE courses, it is time to move on to the second phase of training: learning to train others. This phase of training will equip the student to become a trainer in his or her own right. It is critically important as students make this transition that they follow the example they have been given and facilitate the same courses in the same manner as has been facilitated for them. The temptation for a new facilitator is to fall back into familiar patterns of teaching by lecturing. Doing so, however, will inevitably result in failure to achieve the goal of multiplying servant leaders.

This unit should be studied in its entirety immediately prior to the BEE students beginning their own groups. It provides instruction in the planning and preparation that needs to be done prior to beginning a group, how to choose the right individuals to train, how to start and continue an effective training group, and how to evaluate the effectiveness of your training.

Unit Objective

To equip and build the confidence of a new facilitator to plan and implement an effective training program

Unit Outline

Lesson 10: Preparing an Effective Training Plan (Before you start your group)

Lesson 11: Choosing the Right Students

Lesson 12: Implementing Your Training Plan (Starting your group)

Lesson 13: Evaluating the Effectiveness of Your Training

Lesson 10: Preparing an Effective Training Plan (before you begin your group)

"Begin with the end in mind."
— Stephen Covey

Effective training of servant leaders for the church requires more than the scheduling of a few training sessions. Before scheduling the first training session, it is critical that careful thought be given to the entire training process upon which you are embarking.

In this lesson, you will be led through a process of planning and making the necessary preparations to begin and sustain an effective servant-leader training program.

Lesson Objectives

As a result of this lesson, facilitators will:
- Be able to identify the critical components of an effective servant-leader training program
- Be motivated to give the training of servant leaders the time and attention it deserves
- Respond by writing out a comprehensive plan for training servant leaders in their context

Lesson Outline

Topic 1: Why you must have a plan for training servant leaders

Topic 2: The critical components of an effective plan for training servant leaders

Topic 3: How training servant leaders relates to other ministries of the church

Topic 1: Why You Must Have a Plan for Training Servant Leaders

Your church won't continue growing for very long unless you have a plan for training servant leaders. It is common for churches to grow quite rapidly in their early days, after which growth slows or stops altogether. This slowdown can often be traced to the lack of a plan for training enough servant leaders to care for the growing flock. Jesus Himself expressed concern over the lack of leaders to care for the needs of those who responded to His ministry, and He took immediate action to meet that need (Mt 9:36-10:5).

> **Suggestion for Facilitators:** Use the Step-by-Step Guide to Multiplication and other tools in the BEE World Toolbox to assist your students as they prepare their training plans (see link in Appendix 10). If these tools are not yet available in your or your students' language, consider working with your Country Director to get them translated.

You will also wear yourself out if you don't raise up servant leaders to assist you. The demands placed upon church leaders are many and varied. If a church does not have enough leaders, the leaders it does have will soon be overwhelmed as they faithfully seek to meet the needs of their people. If this situation is not corrected, leaders eventually burn out.

Training Servant leaders won't happen unless you plan for it. The demands of direct ministry always seem more urgent than the need to train others. However, the only way servant leaders will ever be trained is if existing leaders give this ministry the priority it deserves and make time for it. Wise leaders will refuse to give in to "the tyranny of the urgent" by setting in motion a plan for training servant leaders.

Exercise 1

Study Matthew 9:36-10:5, then answer the following questions:
1. What was Jesus' response to the needs of the multitudes who came to hear him preach and be healed?
2. What did he instruct His disciples to do in light of the need for more laborers in God's harvest field?
3. What practical steps did He take to meet the need for more laborers?
4. Discuss the implications of this model for your own ministry.

Topic 2: The Critical Components of an Effective Plan for Training Servant Leaders

Goals and Objectives

A good plan includes long-range goals (10 years or more) as well as short-term (1 year) and medium-range (2-8 year) objectives. Begin by asking God to give you a vision for the number of servant leaders He wants you to have a part in training, both directly (your first generation) and indirectly (your second generation and beyond). Consider not only how many servant leaders your church will need within the next 5-10 years, but how many it will need if it continues to grow as God would desire, perhaps over the next 10 years. Set faith goals that are worthy of the God whom you serve!

Build a plan from the goal God gives you, and establish short-term and medium-range objectives that, if achieved, will likely lead to the realization of your long-range goals. As you set your goals and objectives, keep in mind that we tend to over-estimate what we can accomplish in 1 year, and under-estimate what we can accomplish in 5 or 10 years.

Action Steps

Starting from where you are now, identify specific actions you and your team can take to work towards each objective. You will need to plan what courses you will offer and determine to whom you will offer them. You will need to secure training facilities, and may need to arrange for travel, lodging, and meals for yourself and/or your students, depending on where you conduct the training.

Schedules

Determine a reasonable training schedule. Decide whether you will meet quarterly for one-week intensive training sessions, monthly for one- or two-day sessions, or weekly for half a day (see Appendix 7 for suggestions in this regard). Decide when you will introduce the program and map out all the training sessions required to reach your goals. Schedule all the courses you plan to take your students through over the next several years (see the BEE Curriculum List in Appendix 6). Allow time for your own personal preparation. If you are still being trained when you begin training others (the norm for BEE training), you will need to allow time for both your preparation for the courses you are studying and the courses you will be facilitating. Consider other events and responsibilities that may need to be accommodated as you conduct your training program. There are always adjustments that need to be made at the last minute, but you will be in a much better position to make these adjustments if you have already prepared a schedule than if you have nothing on the calendar. You will also need to communicate the training schedule to those you will be training.

Budget

While the word "budget" usually brings to mind only financial issues, money is only one of three resources for which you will need to budget; the other two are people and "stuff" (materials, facilities, and equipment).

People

Whose help will you need to effectively carry out your training program? If meals will need to be provided during your training sessions, who will prepare them? Who will clean up after meals? If travel and lodging are involved, who will make all these logistical arrangements? Who will print and distribute the materials? Your students can help with some of these details but be careful not to give students responsibilities that will take them out of class (e.g. meal preparation).

Money

Estimate how much each training session will cost and decide how this need will be met. Consider the higher value students will place on the training if they are asked to make a financial investment in it. If the cost would be prohibitive for the students, consider how the church or other interested parties could help. However, be careful not to create a funding system that cannot be replicated and sustained through multiple generations, or multiplication will be hindered.

Stuff

Training materials must be provided for every student, and a plan for them to provide the same materials for their students' needs to be in place if you hope to multiply through succeeding generations. Decide in what form these will be provided (electronic, online, and/or print), and how they will be distributed. This must be done long enough in advance of each training session for the materials to be produced and distributed, and for the students to have time to prepare. Your training venue will need chairs and tables around which small groups can study; a whiteboard with dry erase markers, an eraser, and cleaning solvent. Other materials needed include chart paper with permanent markers and painters tape for hanging charts on the wall. If you plan to use PowerPoint Presentations, a video projector and screen or large-screen TV will need to be provided. If your students plan to use computers, sufficient outlets scattered throughout the training room will be necessary. If online content (e.g. the Internet Biblical Seminary) needs to be accessed, wi-fi access will need to be provided.

Exercise 2

Using the example and template provided in Appendix 8, begin preparing a training plan for your context. Share your plan with others in the class and make note of ideas others have that will be helpful to add to your plan.

Topic 3: How Training Servant Leaders Relates to Other Ministries of the Church

It must be done in addition to your other ministry responsibilities. Training servant leaders is not the only ministry responsibility you will likely have. You will need to manage your time carefully and learn to delegate responsibilities to others to make sure that all of your ministry responsibilities are taken care of.

It must be given adequate priority. As noted previously, attending to other urgent ministry priorities can easily fill our schedules, leaving little or no time for training others. An important principle to keep in mind is that often the most important ministry priorities do not seem to be all that urgent. Given the great need for servant leaders in the church today, it could be argued that training focused on multiplying these is both urgent and important. Whatever the case, it is certainly important, and must be given priority as we plan our schedules.

It can and should be done in the context of total church ministry. The good news is that training servant leaders and fulfilling our other church ministry responsibilities are not mutually exclusive. In fact, it is best if we can involve those we are training in as many other aspects of our ministry as possible. As our students grow in their knowledge, character, and ministry skills, we can also delegate some tasks to them, freeing ourselves up to do the things only we can do. An important principle every facilitator needs to apply regularly is, if someone else can do it, let them!

Exercise 3

Make a chart listing all your ministry responsibilities in one column, the names of students whom you could have accompany and assist you as you carry out those responsibilities in a second column, and the names of students to whom you could delegate some of these responsibilities in the third.

Lesson 11: Choosing the Right Students

Choose the right ones, not just anyone!

Choosing the right students for involvement in the training will be critical in meeting the need of developing qualified servant leaders for the churches within your denomination or group. Much time, energy, and money will be spent in this training, so you want to ensure, to the best of your ability, that the right students have been chosen to participate.

In this lesson, three areas are discussed to help you choose the right students: (1) characteristics of the ideal student; (2) ways to test potential students' ability and commitment before involving them in your group; and (3) the importance of understanding the context and vision for the training.

Lesson Objectives

As a result of this lesson, you will:

- Be able to describe the characteristics of the ideal BEE student
- Be motivated to choose the right students to train
- Be equipped to recruit and effectively screen potential trainees

Lesson Outline

Topic 1: Characteristics of the ideal BEE student

Topic 2: How to Test Ability and Commitment

Topic 3: Understanding the Context and Vision for the Training

Topic 1: Characteristics of the Ideal BEE Student

The desired characteristics described below are to help you think and pray about the right kind of students to be involved in a group of your own. Take time to discuss these characteristics with each potential student. This will show your personal interest in the individual and will help the student understand the kind of person you are looking for to participate in the training. Give the potential student time to think and pray about his or her involvement. Quickly choosing students without thoughtful and prayerful consideration will lead to problems later.

The characteristics are not listed in any particular order, as each is important for the overall success of the student and the group you will lead. Read carefully!

The ideal BEE student:

- Has an existing leadership role that qualifies him to train others—The student's ministry could be in a variety of church leadership responsibilities: pastor, church planter, youth leader, etc. The important thing is that the student be in a position that gives credibility and permission to train others.

- Desires to lead a BEE leadership training group—Each student is required to train others as he is being trained himself. The student's existing ministry should serve as a ready foundation to establish this group.
- Has a good reputation—He or she should be accepted as a leader by others within the church and community.
- Is trustworthy—This is an essential quality to provide a safe environment of open sharing within a group.
- Has a teachable attitude—Even though already teaching others, the student should still have a heart to learn.
- Works well with others—This person is ready to learn in the context of a small group.
- Willing to commit needed time—This will require the student to evaluate present responsibilities in light of adding this new responsibility.
- Academically able to do the course work required—Ideally, the student will have completed high school, but you can consider including *able* students with less formal education.
- Recommended by leadership—Having the support of leaders can be very critical to the student's participation and ability to establish his own group.
- Co-located – He or she needs to live close enough to the training location that travel time and costs do not hinder participation.

Exercise 1

In groups of three or four, discuss why each characteristic is important to the success of the student and the group.

What other suggestions do you have toward helping choose the right students?

Topic 2: Test Ability and Commitment

Some students may express a zeal to be involved in the training and seem to possess the characteristics describe above, but in reality, they are not ready to do all that will be required of them. To help you confirm their ability and commitment, you could do the following:

Plan to meet together as a group three or four times for the purpose of fellowship, prayer, and studying a book of the Bible or some other material available to you. Give an assignment each time. Observe their attendance, ability, and faithfulness to do the work, and their desire to be a part of the group. During this time, it will become evident to some that involvement in such a training group is not for them, or you may see areas in some people that cause you to question their involvement.

Use a pilot course to test their ability and commitment. At the conclusion, you and the student will know better as to whether the student should continue in the group. Be careful not to waste courses on students whom you know from the beginning have neither the ability nor the commitment to participate in the training program (including training others as well as being trained themselves).

Discuss with each student the time required to participate in the training. Show each one a course and describe the amount of study needed. Explain the need and importance to be present in the sessions. Ask the student to evaluate his or her present schedule in light of adding the responsibility of being a part of this group and doing the required work. For many this will require establishing new ministry priorities!

Exercise 2

Discuss the importance of testing the ability and commitment of potential students.

Using a weekly or monthly calendar, have the students write in how they generally use their time during a week and during a month. This should include ministry responsibilities, work (if they have another job), time with family, personal study, school, etc. Then ask them if they believe they have the needed time to be a part of the training. Have them describe when and how that is possible. Does it require a change in ministry priorities?

In groups of three or four have the students discuss the struggles they may have in completing the requirements of the training. What adjustments have they made, or do they need to make?

Topic 3: Understand the Context and Vision for the Training

When you invite students to be a part of the training, you need to help them understand the context and vision for the training. Here are three areas to discuss with them:

Levels of Training

Outline for the students the courses to be taken in each level, the requirements to satisfactorily complete each course before taking the next course, and the time frame for their study.

Academic, Character, and Practical Ministry

Their study will seek to give a balanced emphasis between knowing and understanding the content of a course and applying what is learned in the areas of character and practical ministry skills.

A Multiplying Training System

Each student is required to facilitate the same courses studied to a second-generation group of leaders. Based on the number of students in the first generation, other second-generation groups will be formed, creating a multiplying system of training. The form will vary from location to location, but the outcome will provide greater opportunity for the equipping of leaders for the church.

Exercise 3

Take time to discuss with the students what the course schedule may look like for their situation.

Discuss the importance of balancing the academic, character, and practical ministry in their study.

Review the Introduction to this course, as well as Lesson 3, and discuss the vision for the training.

Exercise 4

Have the students make a list of potential students they would like to challenge to be a part of a second-generation group.

Take five to seven minutes to briefly role-play this challenge with a student. Certainly, it will take longer to do this when actually challenging a potential student to take part in this training, but five to seven minutes should be adequate to communicate the nature of this conversation. Then have the group break into pairs to practice giving this challenge to one another as if each were a potential student. Again, allow five to seven minutes for each person to give the challenge.

Pray together about choosing the right students.

Lesson 12: Implementing Your Training Plan (starting your group)

"Expect great things from God; attempt great things for God"
— *William Carey*

This lesson launches you into your training program. You have learned to facilitate, you have made your plan, you have gathered your resources, and you have chosen your students. Now you are ready to start training them.

You may be overwhelmed by all that is expected of the facilitator and wonder if this is really something you can do. You are not alone with these thoughts; many others have felt the same as you! They, too, struggled with this new role, but with time they gained increasing confidence. Be a patient learner! There will be times when you will think you have failed. Keep pressing forward! You will experience great joy in growing with the students as you guide them through the courses.

In this lesson you will (1) review practical matters related to arranging for a training event, (2) learn how to introduce a new course, (3) learn to facilitate the course to completion, and (4) begin the journey of mentoring your students to learn to facilitate the same course.

Lesson Objectives

As a result of this lesson, you will

- be able to describe the process for starting a BEE training group
- be confident that, with the Lord's enablement, you can do so
- respond by starting your own BEE training group

Lesson Outline

Topic 1: Planning for a Training Event

Topic 2: Facilitating the First Training Event

Topic 3: Facilitating a Course to Completion

Topic 4: Mentoring the Students

Topic 1: Planning for a Training Event

Begin well in advance to prepare for your first training event. Enlist some of your students to help with this. Come early to where you are meeting along with the students who are assisting you to make sure all is in order. The first training event is an important one that will set the tone and environment for future events. If for some reason all is not in order, work hard to change that for the next event. Here is a quick checklist:

- Is the room set up properly to enable good discussion?
- Do you have the needed writing implements for the white board, chart paper, etc.?

- Do you have the right equipment, including power and connecting cords and adapters to project your PowerPoint presentation, if applicable?
- Is the venue well lighted, and temperature controlled?
- Is the food and drink prepared?
- Have sleeping arrangements been made, if needed?

Exercise 1

Take time for questions and discuss any other matters that relate to planning for training events.

Topic 2: Facilitating the First Training Event

The first training event is critical to establishing the framework for beginning a new course. It should promote good attitudes and realistic expectations for the student. It is a time to prepare and motivate the student toward successful completion of a course and deepening of his commitment to you, to the other students, and to the training.

Let's look at a suggested schedule for this important event. It is divided into four sessions with each session requiring approximately an hour and a half to two hours, including breaks. The breaks are important as they allow the students to stretch, refresh themselves, and provide opportunity for lots of unstructured interaction about the course and other matters.

Session 1

Create a welcoming atmosphere: Encouraging a good spirit among the group is very important in making the sessions meaningful and enjoyable. You want each person to feel welcomed and accepted by all. At the very beginning, have the students arrange the room in such a way so they can sit in small groups of four or five. This will create an informal atmosphere that will encourage their interaction.

Then have the students introduce themselves and share briefly about their family and ministry. As the facilitator you should begin this time of sharing. This will help the others share more freely and give them an idea about what to share. If appropriate, take some time to sing a couple of songs they all know. Pray together.

Give a short visionary message about the purpose of this training: You could use 2 Timothy 2:2 and Matthew 28:18-20 as your texts. Not only are these students here to learn for themselves, but they are also committed to teaching others. In an encouraging way, remind the students of the commitment each made to participate in the training. You should mention the importance of being present at all the sessions, doing all the assigned work in the course, being an active participate in the sessions, and teaching a group of their own. Share from your own experience what the commitment required of you.

Give the students some time to ask questions and think through their commitment. Then pray together.

Take a fifteen-minute break!

Session 2

Discuss your plans for the training program, including dates of training events. It would be good for you to have a suggested plan in mind to present to the students. If this is not workable then adjust to meet the needs of the group.

Set the dates for all the training events so students will know well in advance and be able to plan their schedules around those events.

Have each student record the use of his time on a personal calendar or calendar app, including when he will study the course and attend the BEE training events. Look at the charts and have each share with the group how he plans to order his time. Finding time will be difficult for many as their schedules are probably already very busy. They may need help and encouragement in this area. This will be an important exercise!

Discuss recordkeeping: Explain to the students that records will be kept of each one's work. This includes completion of all lessons and related assignments, the exam scores, attendance, other courses completed, and progress in developing the second-generation group. It is very important the students know that you will be diligent in keeping records. Depending on the situation, certificates or diplomas will be issued to the students based on successful work completion, which includes starting a second-generation group. Ask if there are any questions.

Hand out the course material: Give each student a complete copy of the course material to be studied. Give the students ten to fifteen minutes to look through the material. Ask them to hold their questions about the material until after the break.

Take another fifteen-minute break!

Session 3

Introduce the Course: Start the introduction with a short testimony from your own life as to what the study of this course has meant to you. Include several different aspects of how the course influenced your life so they can have a better idea of what to expect in their own study.

Ask the students to read all the introductory material before the first lesson. In some situations, it may be helpful to have them read sections aloud together. Make sure all have completed the reading. Ask for questions and make clarifications as needed.

Have the students complete Lesson 1: Have the students turn to Lesson 1 and explain to them how the lesson is to be completed. Work through the first several topics with them. Then have the students work through all of Lesson 1 in the session. They can work individually or in pairs. The purpose is to make sure they understand how to complete a lesson and to give them a good start. Remind the students that no lesson will be discussed until they have worked through the lesson!

Take another fifteen-minute break!

Session 4

Facilitate Lesson 1: After the students complete the lesson, facilitate the lesson with them. Follow the lesson plan you developed for Lesson 1.

Prepare the students for the next training event: Preview the lessons and assignments to be completed before the next session. Highlight some of the key issues or questions you want them to be ready to discuss. Remind them of the date, time, and place!

Evaluate with the students your time together: Spend a few minutes discussing with the students about your time together. Their input will be helpful for your next training event and will also help them focus on the dynamics of their time together. Evaluation of training events will be discussed more specifically in Lesson 13, Evaluating the Effectiveness of your Training.

Close your time in prayer.

Exercise 2

Take time for questions about leading the first training event.

Topic 3: Facilitating a Course to Completion

The first training event should enable the students to have a good start in their study of a course. Whether you meet in weekly, bi-weekly, monthly, or intensive sessions; the facilitating of the remaining lessons of a course will generally follow the pattern as described above, with the exception of the introductory material.

Each time you facilitate a lesson, your confidence and creativity will grow. Be committed to developing a lesson plan for each lesson. Review often Lesson 8 on preparing lesson plans. Learn from your experiences of facilitating the past lessons. Review often the lessons on Using Questions to Facilitate Learning (Lesson 6), Using Creative Learning Activities (Lesson 7), and Learning to Lead a Small Group Training Session (Lesson 9).

There are many areas to keep in mind as you lead the session and facilitate a course to completion. Here is a checklist of some important ones:

- Develop lesson plans for each lesson!
- Stay on schedule with lessons and dates of sessions.
- Involve the students with helping set up session arrangements.
- Be clear with assignments and what is expected.
- Continue to build relationships with all the students.
- Make mentoring the students an integral part of the session.
- Maintain a good atmosphere in the session.
- Be consistent with keeping records and checking on each student's work (It is highly recommended to appoint a class monitor to help with these tasks).
- Evaluate the session and facilitation with the students.
- Be diligent in solving problems.
- Allow plenty of opportunity for prayer.
- Pass out the materials for the next training session prior to leaving.

Exercise 3

Review the checklist above in a small group. Do you have any questions?

Then make your own checklist of these areas that is easy to review and will serve as a regular reminder for you of what you need to do.

After completing the course take time to get feedback and evaluation from the students. Here are a few suggested questions:

- What were two or three things you learned that significantly impacted your life?
- What did you find most helpful to aid you in your ministries?
- Did the course meet your expectations? Why or why not?
- Are there any questions that are still in your mind about the content of the course?

Topic 4: Mentoring Your Students

Simply stated, a mentor is to be a guide, tutor, counselor, coach, and teacher. Mentoring your students is something you are doing through all your work as a facilitator. And if you take this seriously, it will have significant implications on your role as a facilitator. You want to help each of your students learn to be an able and confident facilitator. To see this become a reality, you will need to keep mentoring your students as a central focus in the leading of the sessions and facilitating the courses.

Because mentoring is such a major area of responsibility, it needs a larger discussion in a separate Unit. Unit 4 will discuss this more at length. It is mentioned in this lesson to remind you that mentoring is to be an integral part of your training program.

Lesson 13: Evaluating the Effectiveness of Your Training

"Experience is not the best teacher; evaluated experience is the best teacher."
— *John C. Maxwell*

Making an evaluation is seeking an answer to the question, "How am I doing?" Evaluating how you are doing at training servant leaders will help you fulfill your responsibilities in the best way possible. This is not only important for you but also for the students you teach and the example you give them.

Sometimes we are not so ready to be evaluated, as we are afraid it may make us look like a failure. However, if the evaluation is done in a meaningful and encouraging way it can be of great value toward becoming successful in what we do. In addition, it helps us see problems more clearly and seek to solve them.

In this lesson you will learn (1) how to evaluate your effectiveness as a trainer, (2) how to gather and make good reports, and (3) how to solve some of the common problems you will face as you seek to train servant leaders.

Lesson Objective

As a result of this lesson, you will

- Be able to evaluate the effectiveness of your training and solve common problems that arise as you begin your training program
- Be motivated to seek honest feedback that will help you improve as a facilitator
- Respond by taking time for evaluation at the end of each training session

Lesson Outline

Topic 1: Guidelines for Evaluating Your Training

Topic 2: Gathering and Making Reports

Topic 3: Solving Common Problem Areas

Topic 1: Guidelines for Evaluating Your Training

As stated above, the purpose of an evaluation is to answer the question, "How am I doing?" Appendix 9, Evaluating Your Training, located at the end of this manual, provides a simple yet comprehensive way to do your evaluation. It is asking questions to provoke your thinking about differing aspects of your training program. The evaluation will help you know in what areas you are doing well, and it will reveal areas that need strengthening or changing.

How often should evaluations be made? In the beginning they should be done often, as this will help you improve your facilitation more quickly. Involving your students in this process will also help them as they begin to teach their own groups. This can serve to build your relationship with them as they see your desire to still learn. One of the best times to do this is at the conclusion of a training session, while everything is still fresh in the minds of both you and your students. Do not become too detailed in the evaluation but take ten to twenty minutes. Look for major areas to improve on for the next time. If you are diligent with the evaluation, you will be encouraged and more confident about your role as a trainer.

If this is the last training session for a course, allow more time, not only for the evaluation, but also to encourage the students to share things they have learned through the course. Here are a few suggested questions to ask:

- What was one of the most significant things you learned through this course?
- What did you find most helpful to aid you in your ministries?

Exercise 1

Read Appendix 9 at the end of this unit.

Discuss the importance of each area in making a good evaluation. Ask if anything else should be added.

Topic 2: Gathering and Making Reports

An important responsibility of every facilitator is to gather and make reports. Few people enjoy this aspect of the ministry, and some even feel that it is unspiritual. While it is true that focusing on results can be done in a prideful manner, the discipline of gathering information and reporting on the results of our ministry is something that is required of us as good stewards. Jesus emphasized this in both his parables (e.g. Matthew 25:14-30) and his teachings (e.g. Luke 16:1-13). The Apostles and church leaders of the New Testament era also apparently kept records and regularly reported on the results of their ministry efforts (see Acts 2:41,47; 4:4; 5:14; 6:1,7; 11:21,26; 14:26-27).

Because the goal of the BEE ministry is to multiply servant leaders for the church, it is important that records be kept, and reports be made to determine if we are being faithful stewards of the ministry God has entrusted to us. Appendix 10 contains several report forms that will greatly assist you in fulfilling this responsibility. Make copies of these forms as needed and use them both to gather and make reports of the results of your ministry.

Topic 3: Solving Common Problem Areas

As you begin facilitating you can be assured that problems will arise! You will often find yourself wondering, "What should I do in this situation?" Having problems is to be expected; you will learn to deal with them as you become more confident in your role as a trainer. Sometimes we create our own problems by not carrying out our responsibilities adequately. Others will come from the students. Still others will arise from situations outside your group over which you have little or no control.

Below is a list of common problem areas and suggested ways to deal with them. If you learn to deal with these problems quickly, firmly, and encouragingly from the beginning, they will become less and less bothersome as you continue facilitating. Also, you will be modeling for your students how they can solve the same problems in their groups. Read the following list carefully and make any notes that come to your mind about these problem areas.

No material. The course material is absolutely essential to facilitating a course. Do **not** attempt to carry on a training program without all the materials being available for all the students as needed for each course. Making this a reality requires advance preparation and organization. Stress the importance of having all required materials available for all students during each meeting with organizing leaders prior to the beginning of the training program. Set up a workable plan for getting the materials for upcoming courses into the hands of the students well in advance. Remember that the students need time to complete their study of the course prior to your coming to facilitate it.

If, having done all in your power to get the materials to the students, they still don't have them when you arrive, be prepared with a clean copy or file that can be sent out to be quick-printed. Once the program is underway, this problem can be avoided by passing out the materials for the next training session at the end of each session.

Meeting place is not good. Often it is very difficult to find what would be the ideal meeting place. Again, advance preparation is critical. Work with the organizers to secure a good meeting place before committing to begin a training program. If, despite your best efforts, you find yourself having to begin in a place that does not provide a good atmosphere for learning, seek out another place. Maybe one of the students has a good idea for a place.

Group is too large. When attempting to facilitate a group of twenty to thirty students the interactive dynamic of a training session is lost. Work hard prior to beginning a group to make sure the organizers understand that the ideal group is 12-16, and in no case should it exceed 20. If, despite your best efforts, you arrive to find yourself faced with too large a group, you will need to negotiate a solution. One possibility is to divide the group into two smaller groups of ten to fifteen. You would then need to facilitate the two groups at different times or possibly another facilitator will be able to help you with the second group. Another possibility is to teach the larger group for one or two sessions, during which time you would work with the organizing leaders to identify the natural leaders among them. You would then invite only these leaders for further training, while assuring the rest that they will all have the opportunity to be trained at the right time by those you have selected.

Facilitator lectures instead of facilitating the lessons. This problem occurs for two main reasons: (1) the facilitator is not committed to the interactive method of instruction, or (2) the facilitator is frustrated with the students not doing their required preparatory work, and is unable to help them change, so returns to the lecture method. The facilitator needs to reevaluate commitment to serving as a facilitator by reviewing Unit 1. Solving the problem of students not doing their work is discussed below.

Wrong choice of students. Following the guidelines given in Lesson 11 will greatly help to prevent this problem. However, there will be cases when you find students in the group who really should not be there. Go over the guidelines in private with the problem student and remind him of his commitment. If you find a student is not willing to follow the guidelines, then that student needs to withdraw from the group.

Frequent student absences. Students need to know that attendance is vital to the satisfactory completion of a course and to the dynamics of the whole group. Only under unusual circumstances, such as, death, family needs, or sickness, should a student miss a training session. Normal ministry activity is not a valid reason. At the beginning of each course, the students need to know the course schedule and to have that written in their schedules. If the student is unable to attend regularly, that student should withdraw from the course. Explain that there will be another opportunity to take the course in the future.

Students do not complete work. If students are not doing the assigned work, remind them that they will not be able to continue with the next course until all work is completed for this course. Check to make sure they clearly understand how the course work is to be accomplished. One way to help correct this problem is to have two people work together on the lessons. They can hold each other accountable for the needed work. If there are a number who are not completing their work, use the training session time for them to do the lesson.

Discussion method too new. This will be one of the greatest challenges for you. Most likely the students have grown up on the lecture method of instruction...even as you did! Explain clearly your role as facilitator and the role of the course material. Help them understand the purpose of using questions and the value of the small group to the learning process. Review with them the material in Lessons 6 and 9 on these two topics.

An important key to their participation will be their completion of the lesson assignments *before* the lessons are discussed. If they have done the work, they will be ready to discuss the lesson. If they have not done the work, they are not ready. In this case, you must use class time for them to complete the lesson. Facilitate the lessons only after the students have completed the lesson!

Education level too low. As mentioned in Lesson 11, it is important to try to determine the student's ability before bringing him into a group. If a student has difficulty doing the work, that student needs to be reminded of the qualifications. Let the student continue in the course, but he needs to be told he cannot continue with the next course. Maybe another student can serve as a tutor to this student for a short time to help with understanding of the material, but this should not become a long-term pattern.

Not understanding how to complete the lessons. This generally happens with students in the very first course. The way of study is new for them and they are not sure how to begin. The key to solving this problem is to have an orientation session prior to the first course, during which you guide the students to work together to complete the first lesson. This will help all the students to know how to complete a lesson and give them greater confidence when they work on their own.

Wandering eyes when taking exams. This is always a difficult area because no one wants to make a bad grade and not look good among his peers. The purpose of the exam is *not* to see how one stands academically among his peers but to help the student with the understanding of the content of the course. Use the exam as a teaching tool by taking time to review answers after the exam has been given and graded. Also, remind the student that the exam counts for only 25% of the total grade. Spread the students as much as possible in the room so the temptation to look at someone else's exam is minimized!

Coming late to training sessions. A student who often comes late to the training sessions needs to be reminded of his responsibility to the other students and to the facilitator. Arriving late to the training session is disruptive, and time is lost. The facilitator should not wait until all are present before starting the training session but should set the example that meetings will start on time. Coming late is sometimes unavoidable, but it should not become a regular practice!

Talking when someone else is speaking. During the training sessions students need to be attentive to one another when someone else is speaking. Active participation is encouraged, but side conversations distract others and show disrespect to the person speaking, whether a fellow student or the facilitator. If someone consistently distracts in this way, it is necessary to speak to that person privately about the problem. Do it in a graceful and firm way!

Ringing and answering of cell phones. All cell phones should be turned off during the learning sessions. The ringing and answering of cell phones are a significant distraction to the overall dynamics of the sessions and show disrespect to the facilitator and the other students. Also, prudence may warrant that no cell phones should be used in any way during the training times.

Exercise 2

In small groups, discuss each of the problem areas and the solutions.

If a group comes up with some other problems areas that are not listed above, they should also come up with suggested solutions.

Unit Four: Mentoring for Multiplication

The great need for servant leaders for the church makes it necessary that we go beyond facilitating courses and training others. We must also mentor those we train to become trainers themselves, and to train their students to train still others. Only in this way, will true multiplication of servant leaders take place. In this unit, we will learn how to mentor those we have trained toward the development of a multiplying training system. Mentoring for multiplication takes us beyond the classroom into the lives and ministries of our students as they seek to start and facilitate groups of their own.

Lesson 14 will equip you to help your students catch a vision for multiplication. In Lesson 15 you will learn how to come alongside your students to effectively encourage and assist them as they start their own groups. Lesson 16 focuses on what is really required if an indigenous church-based multiplying training system is to be established and maintained.

Unit Objective

To provide the facilitator with practical helps in developing a ministry of multiplication, and encouragement toward staying committed to the task of establishing an indigenous church-based multiplying training system.

Unit Outline

    Lesson 14: Helping your Students Catch a Vision for Multiplication

    Lesson 15: Helping Your Students Start New Groups

    Lesson 16: Entrusting the Ministry to Those You Have Trained

Lesson 14: Helping Your Students Catch a Vision for Multiplication

"A leader's role is to raise people's aspirations for what they can become and to release their energies so they will try to get there."
— David Gergen

If your training ministry is to result in the multiplication of servant leaders, you must have a vision to see this happen, and you must pass this vision on to those you train. Casting vision for multiplication must begin very early in the process of training. It should permeate both the classroom and interactions with your students outside the classroom.

In this lesson three important areas will be covered: (1) the importance and "how to" of modeling multiplication, (2) how to communicate your vision for multiplication to your students, and (3) how to help your students develop their own vision for multiplication.

Lesson Objectives

As a result of studying this lesson, you will:

- Be able to describe what it means to model multiplication
- Be able to communicate a vision for multiplication
- Respond by developing a plan for helping their students develop a vision for multiplication

Lesson Outline

Topic 1: Modeling Multiplication

Topic 2: Communicating a Vision for Multiplication

Topic 3: Making Your Vision Take Root

Topic 1: Modeling Multiplication

From the very beginning of the training program—indeed, even before it begins—the facilitator must model a commitment to multiplying servant leaders. The goal of multiplying leaders should be stated clearly from the outset. It should be kept in mind as decisions are made about whom to train. A facilitator who is committed to multiplication will make every effort to focus his energies on training trainers: individuals who are both willing and able to train others.

A facilitator who is committed to multiplication will consistently use transferable materials and training methods, and make sure that those he trains do so as well. He will never do for his students what they can do for themselves. He will not seek to impress his students with his teaching ability but will help them develop their skills as facilitators. He will never use materials or teaching methods that his students do not have access to or will be unable to replicate.

A facilitator models multiplication when he creates and maintains accountability. Paul instructed Timothy to entrust the Word to *faithful* men who would be able to teach others also (2 Tim 2:2, emphasis added).

Students who are not faithful in attendance, completing homework, and starting their own groups should not be allowed to continue participating in the training program.

A facilitator who is committed to multiplication consistently models the attitudes and behaviors he wants to see in his students. He never asks his students to do anything he is unwilling to do himself. Rather, he leads the way, teaching by example.

A facilitator models multiplication by saying "no" to ministry opportunities that would distract from or hinder the work of training trainers. There are many good ministries that will clamor for the facilitator's attention, but if he is to be successful in establishing an indigenous multiplying training system, he must steadfastly refuse to be turned aside from his focus on this goal.

Exercise 1

Make a list of the ministries you are involved in. Evaluate each ministry to determine how it relates to multiplying servant leaders. Does it help or hinder multiplication? Discuss with others in your class how much time should be spent in direct ministry *vs* training and equipping others.

Exercise 2

Compare Luke 9:1-2 with Luke 10:1. How did Jesus model a commitment to multiplication? What can we learn from His example?

Topic 2: Communicating a Vision for Multiplication

Multiplication is impossible without vision. While multiplication takes place automatically in the natural realm, it does not happen in the spiritual realm without intentionality. That is why Jesus was so intentional in the way he went about training His disciples. He modeled an approach to ministry that was focused on multiplication, and His disciples got it. As a result, they went out and "turned the world upside down." We can make a similar impact on our world today, but only if we follow the pattern Jesus gave us.

Exercise 3

Study Matthew 9:36-10:6, then answer the following questions:
1. How did Jesus communicate His vision for multiplication to His disciples?
2. How can we apply the pattern He showed us through this in our own training ministry?

Clearly, one key to passing on a vision for multiplication is to pray for it to happen in the presence of those you are training. Another key is to give your students opportunity to minister themselves, within specific limits that you prescribe (see Jesus' instructions to his disciples before he sent them out in Mt 10:5ff).

Vision for multiplication must be communicated clearly. Don't be vague with your disciples about what you are hoping to accomplish. Share your own goals for multiplying servant leaders for the church. Share how your own vision for multiplication developed.

Vision for multiplication must also be communicated creatively. Use visual aids, cite statistics that underscore the need, and ask questions that stimulate your students to think about both the importance and "how-to's" of multiplication. Share testimonies of others who have been effective in multiplying servant leaders for the church. Better yet, introduce them to such people, and provide opportunities for them to dialog with those individuals.

Communicate vision for multiplication continually. Research shows that when a new concept is introduced to people, they must hear it repeated at least seven times before they really grasp it. Many Christian leaders have never thought about the importance of multiplying servant leaders for the church, much less considered how to do it. Someone has said, "When you're sick of saying it, they're just beginning to get it."

Exercise 4

Brainstorm with your students ways to communicate your vision for multiplication. Here's an idea to get you started:

- Use a map and pray over specific areas where they and their students will train leaders for the church.

Another creative idea can be found in Appendix 4: Paper People Activity.

Topic 3: Making Your Vision Take Root

Merely communicating your vision for multiplication is not enough; you must spend much quality time with those Jesus has given you to train, intentionally seeking to pass it on in a way that will take root and endure.

From the time Jesus chose his 12 apostles until His ascension back into heaven, He was training them to be men of vision. He challenged them to open their eyes and look on the spiritual harvest fields, which were ripe for harvest, and emphasized the need for both sowers and reapers (John 4:35-36). On another occasion He observed, "The harvest is plentiful, but the workers are few," and urged them to "Ask the Lord of the harvest, therefore, to send out workers into his harvest field." (Matt 9:36-37)

He spoke often of the rapid growth of His kingdom, and while He used parables to communicate partial truth to the multitudes, he explained everything to His disciples in private (e.g., Mark 4:30-34). In doing so, He was planting seeds of vision within them that would later bear fruit in the multiplication of leaders for His church.

After His resurrection, and before He ascended to heaven, on numerous occasions Jesus gave His disciples what we have come to know as the Great Commission. We might also describe these commands as a set of Great Visions: "Go and make disciples of all nations…." (Mt. 28:19); "Go into all the world and preach the gospel to every creature." (Mk 16:15); "…you will be my witnesses…to the ends of the earth." (Acts 1:8).

The vision Jesus gave His disciples took root. After His ascension and the outpouring of the Spirit on the day of Pentecost they set about to carry out His commands, and they faithfully worked at this mission until they themselves were taken home.

Exercise 5

If we want our vision to take root, we must train disciples the way Jesus did. Re-read the above paragraphs and create a T-chart that in the left column lists the ways Jesus passed on His vision to His disciples, and in the right column lists similar ways you could pass on your vision for multiplying servant leaders to those you are training. Here are a few ideas to get you started:

How Jesus passed on His vision	How I will pass on my vision
He pointed out the needs of the multitudes and the lack of workers.	I will share statistics and stories that help people understand the need for servant leaders in the church.
He challenged his disciples to pray for more workers to be sent out.	I will pray with my students over the names of people they hope to train.

Lesson 15: Helping Your Students Start New Groups

"My mentor said, 'Let's go do it,' not 'You go do it.' How powerful when someone says, 'Let's!'"
— Jim Rohn

You have successfully started a new group, and you have given them a vision to multiply servant leaders for the church. Now the real test of your commitment to multiplication and effectiveness as a trainer is upon you. Will they be able to do what you have done?

Helping your students begin their own groups is quite a different matter from beginning a group yourself. This is a "next-level" skill that builds upon what you have learned as you started your own group, but also requires additional competencies. It also requires great faith, both in God and in your students. A measure of maturity is also needed; it is somewhat analogous to a parent becoming a grandparent.

> **Suggestion for Facilitators:** This lesson is best facilitated after your students have successfully started their own groups and are preparing to help their students start their groups. Facilitators cannot help someone else develop skills they have not yet acquired themselves. Having your students read this material earlier in the process is valuable, as they need to have a clear view of the whole training process. However, it will be best to work through it with them just prior to the time they will need this information.

This lesson is designed to guide you through this challenging process. It is organized around the widely-used four-step training model:

- I do, you watch
- We do together
- You do, I watch
- I leave, you do

Lesson Objectives

As a result of this lesson, you will:

- Be able to prepare your students to begin their own groups
- Be committed to doing whatever it takes to help your students start their own groups
- Respond by releasing your students to lead their own groups

Lesson Outline

Topic 1: Preparing Your Students to Begin Their Own Groups

Topic 2: Partnering with Your Students to Start New Groups

Topic 3: Supporting Your Students Through the Process

Topic 4: Releasing Your Students to Lead Their Groups

Topic 1: Preparing Your Students to Begin Their Own Groups

Preparing your students to begin their own groups actually begins even before you start your own group. Remember the qualifications for BEE students, as outlined in Lesson 11? The right BEE student: 1) Has an existing leadership role that qualifies him to train others; and 2) Desires to lead his own BEE leadership training group. If you have done a good job of ensuring that your students meet these criteria, you have taken a critical first step to establishing a multiplying training system.

Provide a good model for your students to follow

Most, if not all, of those you train will not have previously trained others, and those who have done so will likely have used the lecture method as their primary training tool. You must therefore show them how to train others before asking them to do it themselves.

Peter exhorted the elders of the church to lead by example (1 Pet 5:3). A facilitator must also lead by example. Those you train may or may not do what you tell them to do, but they will almost always do what you do. Pay close attention to your attitude and your actions; give them an example worth following!

Assess the readiness of your students to start their own groups

Depending on their background, some students may be ready to begin groups early in the training process, and others may require more modeling and equipping before they are ready to do so. A skilled facilitator will discern both the general readiness of the group he is training and individual differences of readiness within the group.

How can we know if our students are ready to start their own groups? Key indicators to look for include:

- A servant heart (as opposed to having an attitude of lording it over others)
- Competence in facilitating interactive learning, as demonstrated through in-class practice facilitation
- Commitment to the 2 Timothy 2:2 approach to multiplying leaders

Don't put this critical step off too long

Because of the challenges inherent in beginning new groups, both trainers and trainees sometimes tend to postpone beginning new groups longer than they should. A general guideline is that your students should be starting their own groups by the second year of the training program.

There are many reasons for this, not the least of which is that people learn best when they begin to teach others. If you really want your students to remember what they learned in your classes, encourage them to teach it to others. If you want them to become proficient in the ministry skills you are seeking to develop in them, give them opportunity to use those skills.

Another important consideration is the urgency of the current situation. The church is growing rapidly around the world, and there is a critical need to rapidly develop new leaders. Unstable political environments in many countries where BEE works may mean that a facilitator's personal ability to continue training a group may be cut off prematurely. Putting off the critical step of helping your students begin their own groups may mean that they will have to do so without your guidance and assistance.

Help your students prepare their training plan

The goal of BEE training is not simply to start new groups, but to multiply leaders. The successful development of a multiplying training system relies upon everyone involved developing and implementing a plan towards that end. It is tempting to just go start a group, but when adequate planning and preparation is not done, it is almost inevitable that the group will become just another Bible study, rather than a leadership training group.

Review Lesson 10 with them and ask them to write out their goals and action steps, outline a training schedule, and establish a budget. Discuss with them how the resources needed for their training program will be provided. Talk about how it will relate to their other ministry responsibilities. If they are overloaded with responsibilities, help them think through how they can cut back on other less important responsibilities to make time for training leaders.

Help your students wisely choose those they will train

Just as you were selective, choosing to train only those who could train others, your students must also learn to be selective. Having the right students in their groups is foundational to a successful multiplication process. Review Lesson 11 with them, and then ask them to make a list of people they think fit the criteria set forth in Topic 1 (Characteristics of the Ideal BEE Student).

The tendency of most beginning trainers is to choose too many students, without giving adequate attention to their qualifications. Impress upon your students the importance of keeping groups small; 12-16 is ideal. Having fewer than that in a group is not a problem, but no group should be allowed to exceed 20 in number. If there are more than 20 who need training, two new groups may be formed, or some can be asked to wait and join the next generation of trainees.

Pray with each student about this critical step in the process. Go through their list with them, praying over each one on their list. Ask questions about the individuals listed, so that you can pray intelligently for them. Ask God to prepare their hearts to respond positively to the challenge your student will give them to be part of his leadership training group.

Exercise 1

Reflect on your own training process as a new BEE facilitator. What was particularly helpful? Where were the gaps? How can you improve the training process for your students?

Topic 2: Partnering with Your Students to Start New Groups

Jesus, the Master Trainer, called His disciples to be "with Him," as well as "to send them out." (Mk 3:15) Initially their time with Him included observing His public ministry and being taught privately. As their training progressed, He delegated increasingly more responsibility to them, giving them counsel about both their attitudes and actions.

In like manner, the Apostle Paul took key disciples he was training along with him as he pursued his ministry, partnering with them to start churches that they would eventually be given full responsibility to oversee.

In vocations that require a high level of skill, novices are required to spend much time as apprentices to experts in the field before being permitted to operate on their own. A student studying to be a medical doctor, for example, must work under the supervision of experienced physicians for some time before being given a license to practice medicine. If this is necessary for those who treat the body, how much more is it necessary for those who minister to the soul?

A BEE facilitator cannot expect that merely facilitating courses will adequately equip his students to train others. He must partner with them in the beginning stages of their training ministry, assisting them to develop their skill as a trainer. There is an art to this, and the wise facilitator will learn to discern how much help is needed, and when offering help to a struggling student may hinder the learning process.

Sometimes, especially when working cross-culturally, it may not be possible for you to personally partner with your students to start new groups. In this case, you should seek to facilitate the development of partnerships with other BEE-trained nationals who could assist your students as they seek to start new groups.

Exercise 2

Study the following passages from the Gospels that show how Jesus partnered with His disciples in ministry. Summarize the events in each passage (some are parallel passages) and identify the principles Jesus followed in each case. Consider the application of these principles to your training situation. How can you partner with your students to start new groups?

References	Events	Principles	Applications
Mk 3:14-15 Lk 6:12-13ff	Appointment of the Twelve Apostles, to be with him and to be sent out to preach and cast out demons. He spent all night in prayer prior to choosing them.	Jesus selected key men to invest His life in training, so that they would multiply His ministry. He chose them after praying much about this decision.	We should choose key disciples to spend extra time with, so that we can send them out to multiply our ministry. We should pray much about who to choose.
Mt 10:1-42 Mk 6:7-13 Lk 9:1-6			
Lk 9:10-11			
Lk 9:12-17 Mt 14:13-20 Mt 15:32-39			

References	Events	Principles	Applications
Luke 10:1-16			
Luke 10:17-24			
Mt 17:14-20			
John 12:20-26			
Jn 21:1-6 (cf Lk 5:1-11, above)			

Topic 3: Supporting Your Students Through the Process of Starting New Groups

Starting new training groups is a challenging process, and your students will need your help to succeed. Here are some suggestions:

Make the content of this course a thread through all your facilitation

Do not teach this course in a few days and think your students have grasped the concepts and practical aspects. As you facilitate other BEE courses, keep applying the principles of this course in your facilitation. Systematically work through this course with your students, introducing each section at the right time, to help them understand what is required to effectively multiply servant leaders and develop the skills needed to do so. Require that your students bring their copy of this course to every session and refer to it regularly. Review key concepts from the course over and over, until they take firm root in your students' minds and hearts.

Provide course material only for individuals enrolled in the training program

The courses are designed for those who are committed to study the material and train others. Do not give extra course material for those not involved in the training program and make it clear that your students are to follow this pattern. Plan ahead to make sure the needed course materials are available when needed. Having the students attempt to start groups without course material will only lead to frustration and discouragement.

Be consistent with accountability and records

This not only applies to the work of your students but also to the work of the students of your students. Use the Multiple-generation Report Form to gather regular reports on how things are going in their groups as well as the groups of their students. Visiting their groups periodically, if possible, will greatly enhance this accountability and record keeping.

Provide regular opportunity to share successes and discuss problems.

As your students begin their second-generation groups, they will be encouraged by the good things that are happening within the group but will need help to solve problems and issues that arise. You can provide some of this, but your students can be a great help to each other as they share their experiences. Give them opportunity for this in each session.

Encourage often!

Your students will need lots of encouragement as they begin their groups. Criticism will only lead to discouragement. Helping to deal with problems in an uplifting manner will lead to building their confidence and success.

Exercise 3

Study the following passages from Acts that relate to how the Apostles supported their disciples through the process of starting new churches. Consider how applying the principles they followed can help you as you support your students through the process of starting new BEE groups.

References	Events	Principles	Applications
Acts 4:23-36 Acts 5:41-42	Disciples pray for boldness and confirming signs after they are persecuted and continue preaching and teaching.	When persecution comes, we should pray for boldness and for God to back us up with miraculous intervention, and not allow persecution to stop us	Let persecution drive you to God for the boldness and backup you need to face it confidently and keep on doing what God has called you to do.
Acts 6:1-7			
Acts 8:12-17,25; Acts 11:19-30			
Acts 9:10-30			
Acts 13:1-5,13			
Acts 14:21-28			
Acts 15:36-41			
Acts 16:1-5			
Acts 18:18-28			
Acts 19:21-22			

References	Events	Principles	Applications
Acts 20:1-6			
Acts 20:13-38			

Topic 4: Releasing Your Students to Lead Their Groups

The fourth step in the training process is one that many trainers find quite difficult to implement: you must release your students to carry on the training ministry without your direct involvement. You have poured your heart and soul into their training, and it is natural to feel protective and want to continue to help them. However, it is critical that at the right time you release your students to carry on the ministry under God's direction and enabling. This will be easier to do if, from the beginning we recognize that the training ministry we are involved in belongs to God, not to us.

A Prerequisite: Holding the ministry with open hands!

Holding the ministry with an open hand before God demonstrates your dependence upon Him in the work He has given to you. This word picture visually expresses your desire to carry out your ministry in a way that will please and honor Him the most. You are no longer focused on success or failure, but rather on staying true to the calling He has given to you and the *manner in which you do the work*. This brings great freedom, confidence, and joy in your ministry.

Exercise 4

Read and reflect on the words of Paul in 1 Corinthians 2: 1-5 and 1 Thessalonians 1:5. How do these verses reflect Paul's dependence upon the Spirit in his ministry to the churches in Corinth and Thessalonica?

From what we read in his letters to these two churches, it seems the ministry outcomes for Paul were considerably different. Read 1 Corinthians 3:1-4 and 1 Thessalonians 1:6-10. What differences do you see?

Read and reflect on 1 Corinthians 3:5-11. According to these verses, how should we view our role in God's work?

Are you holding your ministry tightly or with open hands before God? Discuss how this perspective can be applied in your life and role as a facilitator.

Pray together.

The Process of Releasing Your Students

The process of releasing your students should begin early in their training. From the very first training session, you should make it clear that your goal is to enable them to carry on the ministry without you. You will need to restate this goal many times throughout the entire training process and reinforce it by systematically transferring increasing responsibility to them.

This transfer of responsibility takes place first within the classroom. At first, you will of necessity be doing most, if not all, of the facilitating. However, by the second or third training session, your students should begin doing some of the facilitating, and responsibility should continue to shift from you to the students with each succeeding session, until by the end the students are doing all of the facilitating.

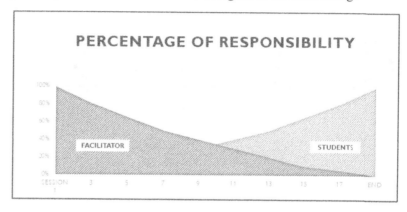

As your students start their own groups, this transfer of responsibility from yourself to the students expands beyond the classroom to encompass the whole training program. Depending on the initiative and capabilities of your students, you may be involved to a greater or lesser extent in helping them start their groups. However, by the end of your personal involvement in training them, they should be willing and able to assume full responsibility for leading these groups, and for keeping the multiplication process going (that is, they should also be prepared to repeat the training process with their own students). This last point will be more fully developed in the following lesson.

Releasing your students does not mean that you are abandoning them. As Jesus spoke of his departure from this world, He assured His followers that He would not leave them without the resources they would need to carry out the commission He had given them (Jn 14:15-18,25-26; 15:26-17; 16:7-15; Lk 24:48; Acts 1:8). As they assumed responsibility for the human side of the work, He sent the Holy Spirit to guide and empower them.

In like manner, as we leave our students, we must empower them to carry out the ministry of multiplying servant leaders for the church. Of course, we can't send the Holy Spirit, as Jesus did, but then again, we don't need to—He is already dwelling in them (Jn 14:16-19; Rom 8:9; 1 Cor 12:13). What we must do is train them to rely upon the power of the Holy Spirit.

We do that first by example, consistently relying upon His power ourselves, and then by teaching them both how to use the Word of God correctly and how to carry out their ministry in the power of the Holy Spirit. The Apostle Paul did just this in his letters to the churches and to the servant leaders he trained. Our faithful teaching of the Word of God and example of ministering in the power of the Holy Spirit will point them to all that they need to carry on the work.

Ultimately, releasing our students is equivalent to empowering them!

Exercise 5

Read John 14-16; Luke 24:48; Acts 1:8; Galatians 5:16,26; Ephesians 5:18-21, and 2 Timothy 1:6-7. Prepare to facilitate a study of these verses, focusing on how the Holy Spirit empowers us for godly living and effective ministry.

Exercise 6

Using Lessons 10-12 as a guide, prayerfully prepare a plan detailing how you will help your students start their own groups. Include faith projections for the number of second-generation groups and students, and a plan for working with your students towards those desired outcomes.

Lesson 15 Answers to Exercises

Exercise 2

References	Events	Principles	Applications
Mk 3:14-15 Lk 6:12-13ff	Appointment of the Twelve Apostles, to be with him and to be sent out to preach and cast out demons. He spent all night in prayer prior to choosing them.	Jesus selected key men to invest His life in training, so that they would multiply His ministry. He chose them after praying much about this decision.	We should choose key disciples to spend extra time with, so that we can send them out to multiply our ministry. We should pray much about who to choose.
Mt 10:1-42 Mk 6:7-13 Lk 9:1-6	Jesus sends the 12 out two by two, after giving them detailed instructions	Jesus limited the scope of his disciples first ministry assignment, and thoroughly instructed them before sending them out	We should limit the scope of our disciples first assignments, and give them detailed instructions what to do
Lk 9:10-11	Jesus tries to go on a retreat with his disciples after they return from their first mission but ends up ministering to the multitudes.	Jesus tried to spend time alone with His disciples after they completed their first assignment, but when other ministry demands prevented this, he was flexible and used the opportunity to let them learn more by observation and helping Him.	We should try to spend time alone with our disciples to debrief, but if other ministry demands prevent this, we should be flexible and have them observe and help as we minister to others
Lk 9:12-17 Mt 14:13-20 Mt 15:32-39	Feeding of the multitudes (twice). In both cases, Jesus challenged his disciples to feed the multitudes, and when they told him they only had insufficient resources, he multiplied what they had and then had them help pass them out and clean up afterwards	Jesus taught his disciples by example that God could miraculously increase their ability to meet people's needs. He challenged their faith, had them invest what they had, and also had them participate in the process of feeding the multitudes.	I need to let those I am training see God miraculously work through me to meet people's needs, challenge them to believe God to do the same through them, and let them invest in and participate in the process.

References	Events	Principles	Applications
Luke 10:1-16	Jesus sends 72 others out two by two, giving them the same instructions He gave the 12 before He sent them out.	As the number of trainees expands, the same instructions given to the first, smaller group should be repeated	Repeat the same instructions to new trainees as you gave to the first ones
Luke 10:17-24	Jesus debriefs the 72 following their mission	Debriefing following mission assignments is important	Debrief every new trainee following his or her first assignment
Mt 17:14-20	Jesus casts a demon out after his disciples had failed to do so, then explains that their failure was due to lack of faith	It is important to limit the effect of your trainees' failures, and to use such times as an opportunity for additional training	When my trainees fail, back them up and afterwards teach them what they need to know so they won't fail in that same way again
John 12:20-26	Jesus uses the occasion of Greeks wanting to see him to talk about the multiplying impact of his death and applies it to the need for his disciples to view their life in the same way.	Requests for ministry that don't fit your current focus can give opportunity to teach about priorities.	We don't need to respond to every request, but instead should use such requests to teach our disciples about priorities in ministry.
Jn 21:1-6 (cf Lk 5:1-11, above)	Jesus performs the same miracle as He did when He called Peter (and other disciples) as He prepares to restore him (and them)	Jesus wanted to remind Peter and the other disciples that the same power that drew them to Him at the first was still available, even though it seemed all was lost	When your disciples are tempted to give up, do things to remind them that God's power is still available to them.

Exercise 3

References	Events	Principles	Applications
Acts 4:23-36 Acts 5:41-42	Disciples pray for boldness and confirming signs after they are persecuted and continue preaching and teaching.	When persecution comes, we should pray for boldness and for God to back us up with miraculous intervention, and not allow persecution to stop us	Let persecution drive you to God for the boldness and backup you need to face it confidently and keep on doing what God has called you to do.
Acts 6:1-7	Deacons are appointed	Physical needs among God's people need to be met without distracting leaders from the ministry of the Word and prayer	Organize and delegate instead of trying to meet every need yourself
Acts 8:12-17,25; Acts 11:19-30	Samaria evangelized, and churches planted, Peter and John are sent to help Philip; church at Antioch established, Barnabas sent to help, and he gets Paul to help.	When new areas are evangelized, leaders need to give attention to see that the church is properly established	Assign mature leaders to assess new groups and assist in their development.
Acts 9:10-30	Ananias, other disciples at Damascus, and Barnabas help Saul develop in his early days as a believer	God will prompt key leaders and other disciples to assist in the development and effective deployment of new leaders	Be sensitive and obedient to God's promptings to come alongside a new key believer
Acts 13:1-5,13	Barnabas and Saul sent out from Antioch; Paul soon becomes the leader of the team	Sometimes leadership switches from one person to another	Be willing to let someone you have mentored become your leader.
Acts 14:21-28	Paul and Barnabas return to appoint elders and encourage the young churches	New churches need elders and encouragement	Appoint leaders and encourage new groups
Acts 15:36-41	Paul and Barnabas split; two teams formed, churches strengthened	Division happens, and should result in more ministry, not less	Don't let divisions discourage or stop you

References	Events	Principles	Applications
Acts 16:1-5	Timothy recruited to join the team and accompanies Paul and Silas	Promising young men need to be recruited and developed into strong leaders	Look for "Timothies" and be willing to invest in them.
Acts 18:18-28	While Paul continues his itinerant ministry, Priscilla and Aquila (Paul's disciples) disciple Apollos (next generation training)	Paul discipled Priscilla and Aquila while making tents, and they discipled Apollos.	Training done even when seemingly distracted from ministry can result in generational multiplication
Acts 19:21-22	Paul sends Timothy and Erastus to Macedonia	Those you have trained will expand your ministry	Deploy those you've trained to follow up on groups you can't go to yourself
Acts 20:1-6	Paul travels with a large team of co-workers	Paul was carrying a large gift for the poor saints in Jerusalem, and doubtless felt it would be good to have a large team to guard the money.	Travel together with teams when appropriate
Acts 20:13-38	Paul gives a final charge to the Ephesian elders	There is a time to recognize your ministry to a group is ending, and to bring it to a fitting conclusion.	Entrust those you've trained to God's care!

Lesson 16: Entrusting the Ministry to Those You Have Trained

As iron sharpens iron, so one man sharpens another.
— Proverbs 27:17 (NIV)

We come now to the final lesson in this course. If you are previewing the course, we hope you have seen that the goal of multiplying servant leaders is attainable; there is a path that, if followed carefully and diligently, will lead to that end. If you have come to this point in your study and application of the course, you have already been walking that path for a significant amount of time, and hopefully have already begun to see servant leaders multiplied.

You have learned to lead through serving, and trained others to do the same. You have faithfully facilitated multiple courses for the same students, over a significant amount of time. You have trained your students to facilitate these same courses for others. You have passed on your vision for multiplication to your students and helped them start their own groups. Now it is critical that you do one more thing: you must entrust the ministry to those you have trained.

Lesson Objectives

As a result of studying and applying this lesson,
- You will be able to describe the process of entrusting the ministry to those you have trained
- You will be challenged and encouraged to release your students to carry on the ministry without you
- You will have assisted your students to develop a plan for sustaining this important ministry for the foreseeable future.

Lesson Outline

Topic 1: How Jesus entrusted the ministry to those He trained
Topic 2: How the Apostle Paul entrusted the ministry to those he trained
Topic 3: How you can entrust the ministry to those you have trained

Topic 1: How Jesus Entrusted the Ministry to Those He Trained

God has not left us without guidance with regard to this final important task in our training ministry. As we look at the example of Jesus, we see a very intentional process of entrusting the ministry to those He had trained to lead it.

He Instructed Them

In all four of the gospels, as well as the first chapter of Acts, we find Jesus giving very specific instructions to both the twelve and the larger group of disciples concerning their responsibilities after He was gone.

Foremost among these instructions was the Great Commission. Jesus was very clear: those He had trained were to carry on His mission. There were not to go back to doing the same things they had been doing prior to their call to follow Him. He had trained them to make disciples, and that is what they were to focus their energies upon for the rest of their lives.

QUESTION 1

In your Life Notebook, compare and contrast the five accounts of the Great Commission, as recorded in Matthew 28:18-20, Mark 16:15, Luke 24:46-49, John 20:21, and Acts 1:8. Discuss what these instructions meant for those to whom they were originally given, and what they mean for us today. Evaluate your own ministry in light of these commands; are you faithfully working at carrying out the Great Commission?

He Warned Them

It is striking as you read the accounts of Jesus' last days with his disciples how often he spoke of the difficulties they would encounter after His departure. Specifically, He warned them not to be misled by false prophets (Matt 24:4,11), and that they would be hated, persecuted, and killed (Matt 24:9-10: Luke 23:12-17; John 15:18-21).

Even within the ranks of the original 12 apostles, one proved to be a false apostle.

QUESTION 2

Read John 13:18-30 and 17:12, then answer the following questions in your Life Notebook:
- Why was Judas included among the original 12 apostles?
- How did Judas' betrayal affect Jesus?
- How did Jesus deal with the challenges that Judas presence among the twelve presented?

Jesus lovingly, but firmly dealt with Judas, not allowing him to hinder the purpose of God. He ultimately was excluded from the apostolic band and served as a warning to all of the folly of allowing greed and personal ambition to supplant commitment to leading as a servant.

If even one of the men whom Jesus trained betrayed him, we should not be surprised if there are some we train who turn out to be false brothers or sisters. It is important that we take Jesus' warnings seriously and deal appropriately with those Satan "plants" among the believers to try to hinder God's purposes from being accomplished.

He Prayed for Them – And for All Who Would Believe as a Result of Their Testimony

Knowing that His disciples would face great difficulties following His departure, Jesus prayed for them (John 17:6-19). He also prayed for those that would believe because of their testimony, that is, all believers everywhere, from that time forward (John 17:20-26).

QUESTION 3

Read John 17. In your Life Notebook, answer the following questions:
- How did Jesus describe His relationship with the twelve?
- How did He describe and evaluate His ministry to them?
- What specific requests did He make of the Father for them, and for those who would come to believe through their testimony?
- What seems to have been His main concern as He prayed for them?
- What does this teach us about how we should pray for those we train?

Jesus also prayed specifically for Simon Peter, that his faith would not fail (Luke 22:31). Although Peter did deny Christ three times, Jesus' prayer for him was clearly answered, as he repented of these sins, and went on to become a powerful preacher of the gospel and leader of the early church.

He Restored Those Who Stumbled

We often focus on Peter's denial of Christ, but we should remember that all the disciples forsook Jesus and fled when He was arrested in the Garden of Gethsemane (Matthew 26:56). The account of how Jesus restored them, with a particular focus on Peter, is recorded in John 21.

QUESTION 4

Read John 21:1-14, as well as Luke 5:1-11, and then answer the following questions in your Life Notebook:
- Why do you suppose Jesus repeated the same miracle He performed when He first called several of the disciples to follow Him?
- What was the impact of this miracle on the disciples?

QUESTION 5

Read John 21:15-19, then answer the following questions in your Life Notebook:
- Why did Jesus ask Peter three times if he loved Him?
- What did Jesus instruct Peter to do?
- What did He warn him would happen to him in the future?

QUESTION 6

Read John 21:20-22. Why do you suppose Jesus rebuked Peter so directly when he asked about "the disciple whom Jesus loved"? Record you answer in your Life Notebook.

QUESTION 7

What insights does John 21 give us into how Jesus responds when we stumble? What insights does it give us about how we should treat our disciples when they fail? Record you answer in your Life Notebook.

If the disciples of Jesus stumbled, we should not be surprised when those we train stumble. Some, like Judas, may prove to not have been true disciples at all. Others, like Peter, will deeply disappoint us. However, if we faithfully instruct our disciples, give them warning, pray for them, and seek to restore them when they stumble, the majority will go on to bring glory to God by accomplishing the ministry entrusted to them.

He Left Them

There was a definite end-point to the personal ministry of the Incarnate Christ to his disciples. He left the earth and ascended to the Father (Acts 1:9). The ministry was now in their hands.

He did not leave them alone, however. He sent the Holy Spirit to empower them to carry out the ministry He had entrusted to them (Acts 1:4-5, 8)

As we seek to entrust our ministry to those we have trained, like Christ, we need to give them careful instruction, warn them clearly concerning the difficulties they will face, pray with and for them, and be there to help them up when they stumble – but only for a season. There comes a time when, like Christ, we must leave them. We do not leave them alone, however, for the Holy Spirit indwells them, and will empower them for the ministry we have entrusted to them.

Topic 2: How the Apostle Paul Entrusted the Ministry to Those He Trained

The Apostle Paul also set an example for us by entrusting the ministry to those he trained. His pattern for doing so closely followed that of the Lord Jesus Christ.

He Instructed Them

Like Jesus, Paul gave those he trained much specific instruction in how to carry out their ministry, both before and after they were deployed. In the case of Timothy and Titus, we have these instructions preserved in the pastoral epistles (1 & 2 Timothy, Titus).

QUESTION 8

Read 1 Timothy, then match the passages in the left column with the instructions in the right column:

Scripture	Instructions
1 Timothy 6:20	Keep away from love of money; instead, pursue righteousness, godliness, faithfulness, love, endurance, and gentleness
1 Timothy 4:11-16	Protect what is entrusted to you
1 Timothy 6:11-15	Instruct certain people not to spread false teaching, and focus your instruction on love that comes from a pure heart, a good conscience, and a sincere faith
1 Timothy 1:18-19	Fight the good fight; hold firmly to faith and a good conscience
1 Timothy 1:3-5	Command and teach good doctrine; don't let anyone look down on you because you are young; set a good example; be conscientious about how you live and what you teach

In Paul's second letter to Timothy he repeats some of the instruction he gave him in the first letter (compare, for example 1 Tim 4:14 with 2 Tim 1:6). This underscores the importance of repetition in training others. Our students will often not "get it" the first time we teach them something, and we should be prepared to repeat these instructions until they do.

Paul also introduces some new themes in 2 Timothy and expands on others that he only touched upon in 1 Timothy.

QUESTION 9

Read 2 Timothy 1:8; 2:3; 4:5 and note the themes that are common to them.

QUESTION 10

Now read 2 Timothy 2:15; 3:14-17; 4:1-2 and record the themes.

Paul gives many of the same instructions to Titus, most notably the instruction to entrust the things he had taught him to people who will be able to train others (Tit 2:1-8). Interestingly, in his instructions to Titus, he relates the multiplication process specifically to women and the family structure within the church (Tit 2:3-4).

Suggestion for facilitators: You may find it helpful to remind your students of the four generations of training we see in II Timothy 2:2 (Paul, Timothy, faithful men, others also), and then have them construct a chart of the multiple generations outlined in Titus 2:1-8.

Lesson 16: Entrusting the Ministry to Those You Have Trained

QUESTION 11

Compare 2 Timothy 2:2 with Titus 2:1-8, then answer the following questions:
- Which specific groups of people was Titus instructed to directly teach or train (Tit 2:2-3,6)?
- How was Titus to train these groups (vv.7-8)?
- What groups were to be trained by others (v.4)?
- Why do you suppose Paul specifically excluded these individuals from Titus' direct training ministry (cf 1 Tim 5:2)?

Clearly, Paul found it necessary to give very specific instructions to those he trained as he was in the process of entrusting the ministry to them. These instructions were different for different men, no doubt because of varying needs within their particular ministry situation.

He Warned Them

Just as Jesus warned his disciples to watch out for false teachers and to be prepared to endure persecution, Paul warned his disciples concerning the same things. In his final meeting with the elders of the church in Ephesus (Acts 20:17-38), Paul recounted his own sufferings and then warned them to "²⁸ Watch out for yourselves and for all the flock of which the Holy Spirit has made you overseers, to shepherd the church of God that he obtained with the blood of his own Son. ²⁹ I know that after I am gone, fierce wolves will come in among you, not sparing the flock. ³⁰ Even from among your own group men will arise, teaching perversions of the truth to draw the disciples away after them. ³¹ Therefore be alert, remembering that night and day for three years I did not stop warning each one of you with tears." (Acts 20:28-31)

We also find similar warnings to Timothy and Titus, along with instructions about how to deal with those who sow discord by promoting false teaching and ungodly living in the church.

QUESTION 12

Match the passages on the left with the instructions on the right

Scripture	Instructions
1 Timothy 5:19-20	Refute legalism and reject myths as a good servant of Christ Jesus
1 Timothy 4:1-7	Silence rebellious people, rebuking them sharply, that they may be healthy in the faith
2 Timothy 4:1-5	Avoid ungodly people who maintain the outward appearance of religion but have repudiated its power
Titus 1:10-14	Preach the Word, reprove, rebuke, and exhort with complete patience and careful instruction.
2 Timothy 3:1-5	Don't accept an unconfirmed accusation against an elder, but rebuke those guilty of sin before all, as a warning to the rest

Paul also specifically warned Timothy about those who deserted and opposed him, telling him to be on his guard against the latter (2 Timothy 4:10,14-15).

He Prayed for Them

Paul spoke of his unceasing prayer for Timothy in 2 Timothy 1:3. In his letters to the churches he had planted and the leaders he had trained, Paul includes a number of prayers that serve as a model for how to pray for our disciples.

EXERCISE 1

Copy the following list of the prayers of Paul, place the copy in your Bible, and use these prayers as guides as you pray for those to whom you are entrusting the ministry:

Romans 1:8–10	1 Thessalonians 2:13–16
Romans 15:5–6	1 Thessalonians 3:9–13
Romans 15:13	1 Thessalonians 5:23–24
1 Corinthians 1:4–9	2 Thessalonians 1:3
2 Corinthians 13:7–9	2 Thessalonians 1:11–12
Ephesians 1:15–23	2 Thessalonians 2:16–17
Ephesians 3:14–21	2 Thessalonians 3:2–5
Philippians 1:3–6	2 Thessalonians 3:16
Philippians 1:9–11	2 Timothy 1:3–7
Colossians 1:3–14	Philemon 4–7
1 Thessalonians 1:2–3	

He Sought the Restoration of Those Who Stumbled

While earlier in his ministry Paul was unwilling to give John Mark a second chance (see Acts 15:37-38), towards the end of his ministry he re-affirmed him as a valued co-worker (2 Tim 4:11). Paul also urged the church at Corinth to restore one of their members who had sinned and had to be disciplined after he repented (2 Cor 2:5-11), and he instructed the Galatians to restore those caught in any sin (Gal 6:1).

EXERCISE 2

Read Acts 15:36-41 and 2 Timothy 4:9-18. Record your observations on how Paul dealt with interpersonal conflicts in the context of his ministry relationships. Do you agree with the way he handled these? Why or why not? How would you have handled them?

Unlike our Lord, Paul was an imperfect example. Nevertheless, we can learn much from his example as one who sought to glorify God in all he did.

He Left Them

Paul's pattern throughout his ministry was to train servant leaders for a season, and then entrust the ministry to them as he moved on to new fields. He refers specifically to leaving Timothy in Ephesus (1 Tim 1:3) and Titus in Crete (Tit 1:5). Later, he wrote in moving terms concerning his impending death:

> ⁶ For I am already being poured out as an offering, and the time for me to depart is at hand.

⁷ I have competed well; I have finished the race; I have kept the faith!

⁸ Finally the crown of righteousness is reserved for me. The Lord, the righteous Judge, will award it to me in that day—and not to me only, but also to all who have set their affection on his appearing. (2 Tim 4:6-8)

We will all, at some point, be called upon to leave those we have trained. It is important that we do a good job of entrusting the ministry to them, so that when we leave, they can carry it on effectively without us.

Topic 3: How We Can Entrust the Ministry to Those We Have Trained

As we have seen, Jesus gave us a clear pattern for entrusting the ministry to his disciples. The Apostle Paul followed that pattern, and so should we. The pattern that served the early church so well, multiplying servant leaders to serve a rapidly-expanding church, will serve us well today, but only if we follow it.

We Must Instruct Them

As we have seen, both Jesus and Paul found it necessary to give very specific instructions to those they trained as they were entrusting the ministry to them. In like manner, we must leave those we train with specific instructions that will enable them to effectively carry on the ministry without us.

They must be instructed to keep the Word of God central in their ministry. They must be able to handle the Word of God accurately and be committed to testing all teaching by the Word of God. In other words, BEE training is first and foremost *biblical*.

They must be instructed to keep their ministry *church-focused*. The church is God's ordained organism whereby He accomplishes His work in the world, and through which church leaders are to be trained.

They should also be instructed to serve church leaders whose access to pastoral training is limited. This limitation may be due to government restrictions, cultural opposition, or religious oppression, or it may be due to issues like geography, poverty, economics, or civil war. BEE training is designed primarily for those leaders who have *restricted access* to training.

They must be instructed to facilitate growth in biblical knowledge, godly character, and ministry skills. The goal is not to transfer knowledge alone, but to develop godly, capable servant leaders. BEE training is *whole person training*.

They must be instructed to practice and promote *indigenization*. Wherever BEE goes, nationals (local people) should be progressively equipped to own and implement the training ministry. The BEE ministry should be self-supporting, self-governing, and self-propagating.

They should also be instructed to use a transferable, Bible-centered curriculum, and a transferable training method (facilitation). *Transferability* is a critical component of the BEE training ministry.

They must be instructed to multiply servant leaders through succeeding generations. *Multiplication* should be the goal of every BEE training ministry and can be achieved by carefully following the principles outlined in this manual.

Finally, they must be instructed in *teamwork*. The BEE ministry is best served by a team working together in unity of mission and spirit, growing in faith, zealous for God's purpose, while demonstrating the fruit of the Spirit.

We Must Warn Them

Enemies of the gospel abound, and we must equip those we train to stand firm when these enemies come against them. These enemies may be obvious, such as those who persecute the church, or they may be covert, such as the false teachers who creep in to draw disciples away into error.

Behind these human enemies are demonic principalities and powers, and we must equip our disciples with the full armor of God to overcome them (Eph 6:10-20). We must teach them to rely on the freedom they have in Christ and the power of the Holy Spirit. We must teach them by example to be careful, but not fearful.

> [7] For God did not give us a Spirit of fear but of power and love and self-control.
>
> [8] So do not be ashamed of the testimony about our Lord or of me, a prisoner for his sake, but by God's power accept your share of suffering for the gospel. 2 Timothy 1:7-8

We Must Pray for Them

Training servant leaders for the church is a spiritual ministry, and to be effective it must be constantly undergirded by prayer. Develop and maintain a prayer list of all those you train, and faithfully uphold them in prayer as and after you entrust the ministry to them. Keep in touch as you are able, so that you can pray with understanding. Respond to the promptings of the Holy Spirit, so that you can effectively lift them up even when you do not know, from a human perspective, what is going on in their lives and ministries.

We Must Seek to Restore Those Who Stumble

It is easy to get discouraged and give up on people when they don't respond to our ministry as we would like them to. At such times we must remember that God never gives up on us, and He expects us to show the same grace and mercy to others that we have received from him.

We must follow the biblical instructions concerning how to approach someone who has fallen into sin or wandered from the path and take the initiative to seek their restoration to fellowship with God and His people. Sometimes rebuke is called for; at other times a gentler approach is needed. Let us not fall short of our responsibility to do everything we can to restore a brother or sister who has stumbled.

We Must Leave Them in God's Hands

A wise leader knows when to leave. Often the development of new leaders is hindered by a leader who holds onto the reigns of the ministry too long or too tightly. It is tempting for some to feel that those they have trained are not ready to assume responsibility for the ministry long after it should be released to them.

The real test comes when someone to whom we are entrusting the ministry wants to do things differently than we did them. At such a point, we may give counsel, but we need to leave the decisions about such things in their hands. The indigenization process inevitably involves some adaptation of the BEE methodology to the culture.

Ultimately, the BEE ministry belongs to God, not to us, and in the end, we need to not only entrust the ministry to those we have trained but entrust them to God.

And now I entrust you to God and to the message of his grace. This message is able to build you up and give you an inheritance among all those who are sanctified. (Acts 20:32)

Lesson 16 Answers to Questions

QUESTION 1: *Your answer should be similar to the following:*

Reference:	Matthew 28:18-20	Mark 16:15	Luke 24:46-49	John 20:21	Acts 1:8
Preface	All authority has been given to me in heaven and on earth	He rebuked them for their unbelief and hard hearts	Scripture prophesied Christ's death and resurrection as well as the proclamation of the gospel to all nations, beginning from Jerusalem	Peace be with you	You will receive power when the Holy Spirit has come upon you
Main Command or emphasis	Go, make disciples	Go, preach the gospel	You are witnesses	Just as the Father has sent me, I also send you	You will be my witnesses
Scope	All nations	Every creature	All nations		In Jerusalem, Judea, Samaria, and to the farthest parts of the earth
Other instructions	Baptize, teach		Stay in the city until you have been clothed with power from on high.		
Associated promises	I am with you always, to the end of the age	Signs and wonders will accompany those who believe	I am sending the Holy Spirit	If you forgive anyone's sins, they are forgiven; if you retain anyone's sins, they are retained	This same Jesus…will come back in the same way you saw him go into heaven

For the disciples to whom Jesus originally gave these instructions, these commands meant that they were to wait in Jerusalem until the Holy Spirit was given, preaching there first, and then going out to the surrounding area and across cultural and national boundaries to spread the gospel and make disciples of everyone who responded.

For us, it means that we must go in the power of the Holy Spirit and preach the gospel to everyone who will listen, among every people group. We are to make disciples of all who respond by baptizing them, planting churches, and teaching them to obey all Christ's commands. We are to continue doing this until Jesus returns, or until He takes us home.

QUESTION 2: *Your answer should be similar to the following:*
Judas was included among the 12 so that the Scripture (specifically the prophecy of Ps 41:9) would be fulfilled. Judas' betrayal deeply distressed Jesus but did not deter Him from His appointed task. Jesus did not shame Judas before the other apostles, but He removed him from among them (John 13:27) before his final, most intimate discourse with them (John 13:31-16:33)

QUESTION 3: *Your answer should be similar to the following:*
In John 17, Jesus described His relationship with the twelve as one of mutual commitment, ordained by God, and characterized by faith and obedience on the part of the disciples (vv.6,8). His ministry to them included revealing the Father's name to them (v. 6a), giving them the words the Father gave Him (v.7), praying for them (v.9), keeping them safe (v.12), and giving them perfect joy (v.13). He prayed that they might be kept safe from the evil one (v.15), and that they would be set apart in the truth (v.17). He prayed for those who would believe through their testimony, that they would be one with one another and with the Father and Himself (vv.20-23). He also prayed that they would be with Him where He would be and see His glory (v.24). His main concern for them seems to be that they would follow through on the things He had taught them, and fully experience all that God had in store for them. We should pray these same kinds of things for those we train.

QUESTION 4: *Your answer should be similar to the following:*
Jesus clearly wanted to remind Peter and the other disciples that He had called them to become fishers of men, and that He had the power to enable them to succeed at this task. The impact of this miracle no doubt was to greatly encourage and increase their faith.

QUESTION 5: *Your answer should be similar to the following:*
While the Scripture does not tell us why Jesus asked Peter three times if he loved Him, it seems likely this was to affirm to Peter that He still desired a close relationship with him, despite his three denials of Christ (Jn 18:17,25-27). Jesus instructed Peter to feed His lambs (v.15), shepherd His sheep (v.16), and feed His sheep (v.17). He also commanded him, "Follow Me" (v.19). He warned him that he would be persecuted and ultimately martyred (vv 18-19).

QUESTION 6: *Your answer should be similar to the following:*
Jesus wanted Peter to focus on his own relationship with Christ, not on that of others. Peter's earlier boast that his loyalty to Christ exceed that of the other disciples (cf Mt 26:33; Mk 14:29; Jn 13:37) suggests that he may have had an unhealthy tendency to compare himself to others. Jesus question, "Do you love me more than these?" (Jn 13:15) also seems to focus on helping Peter deal with this issue.

QUESTION 7: *Your answer.*

QUESTION 8

Scripture	Instructions
1 Timothy 6:20	Instruct certain people not to spread false teaching, and focus your instruction on love that comes from a pure heart, a good conscience, and a sincere faith
1 Timothy 4:11-16	Fight the good fight; hold firmly to faith and a good conscience
1 Timothy 6:11-15	Command and teach good doctrine; don't let anyone look down on you because you are young; set a good example; be conscientious about how you live and what you teach
1 Timothy 1:18-19	Keep away from love of money; instead, pursue righteousness, godliness, faithfulness, love, endurance, and gentleness
1 Timothy 1:3-5	Protect what is entrusted to you

QUESTION 9: *Your answer should be similar to the following:*
Endure hardship or suffering

QUESTION 10: *Your answer should be similar to the following:*
Study, preach, and teach the Word

QUESTION 11: *Your answer should be similar to the following:*
Titus was instructed to directly teach older men, older women, and younger men. He was to train them by his example as well as by sound teaching. Older women were to train the younger women. Paul may have given Titus this instruction to guard against an inappropriate relationship developing between himself and one of the younger women in the church.

QUESTION 12

Scripture	Instructions
1 Timothy 5:19-20	Refute legalism and reject myths as a good servant of Christ Jesus
1 Timothy 4:1-7	Don't accept an unconfirmed accusation against an elder, but rebuke those guilty of sin before all, as a warning to the rest
2 Timothy 4:1-5	Avoid ungodly people who maintain the outward appearance of religion but have repudiated its power
Titus 1:10-14	Preach the Word, reprove, rebuke, and exhort with complete patience and careful instruction.
2 Timothy 3:1-5	Silence rebellious people, rebuking them sharply, that they may be healthy in the faith

Appendix 1: BEE World Core Values

BEE World's mission is to help the church fulfill the Great Commission by providing biblical training that results in the multiplication of servant leaders with priority given to countries with limited access to training.

CORE VALUES

1. Biblical

BEE World believes that the core of training church leaders rests upon the Bible; Scripture being both inerrant and infallible.

2. Church Focused

BEE World believes that the church is God's ordained organism whereby He accomplishes His work in the world and through which we train church leaders.

3. Restricted Access

BEE World believes in serving church leaders who face Restricted Access to pastoral training due to government, cultural, or religious oppression. We also serve those in strategic fields that face severely Limited Access to training due to issues like geography, poverty, economics, and civil war.

4. Whole Person Training

BEE World believes that training should facilitate growth in skill, knowledge, and character enabling and molding students to become sacrificial, humble Servant leaders expressed in godly leadership.

5. Indigenization

BEE World trains nationals to train their own. Nationals should be progressively equipped to own and implement the training ministry, becoming self-supporting, self-governing, and self-propagating.

6. Transferability

BEE World believes training is best reproduced through a transferable, Bible-centered curriculum that enhances multiplication and utilizes facilitation as the normal teaching method.

7. Multiplication

BEE World believes that the training process should be designed to multiply to successive generations. (2 Timothy 2:2; Matthew 28:19-20).

8. Teamwork

BEE World believes that our ministry is best served by a team working together in unity of mission and sprit, growing in faith, zealous for God's purpose, while demonstrating the fruit of His Spirit.

Appendix 2: Educational Methodology

In addition to our core values, we hold to an Educational Methodology that is driven by 2 Timothy 2:2 and defined by the following characteristics.

1. Training While Ministering

BEE World trains nationals as they serve in their existing ministries, without removing them from their ministry context.

2. Facilitation Approach to Learning

BEE World believes that facilitation is the best teaching approach for guiding learners to think, conclude, and apply course material. This stimulates whole-person training and equips them for multiplication as they practice this method. The teacher is a facilitator of learning rather than a transmitter of information.

3. Bible-Centered Curriculum

BEE World designs Bible-centered curriculum to be a critical component in our mission to equip nationals to equip others. Each course is designed for interactive learning and becomes the professor, the core guide for biblical information and doctrine.

4. Relational Mentoring

BEE World believes that the development of Christlike character is enhanced within the context of positive, ongoing, interpersonal relationships where modeling takes places between teacher and students.

5. Student Selection

BEE World believes that students selected for training should be involved in church ministry, possess the educational and spiritual capacity for the studies, and be ones whom their church leadership trusts to train other.

6. Cultural Contextualization

BEE World believes that training should be culturally appropriate and credible to effectively develop servant leaders for churches in any given country.

7. Evaluation and Adaptation

BEE World believes that effective training systems incorporate continuing evaluation, adaptation, and quality control.

8. Healthy Partnerships

BEE World believes that the most effective approach to equipping generations of leaders is through healthy and effective partnerships with churches, networks, and like-minded agencies—both western and indigenous. BEE World strives to develop loving, selfless cooperation between evangelical believers and groups based upon evangelical values and integrity.

Appendix 3: Time in a Jar Illustration

Facilitator Note: The demonstration itself should take about 10 minutes, or perhaps 15-20 with an interpreter. It will take longer if you let a student practice it after you have led through parts 1 and 2—but this is highly recommended, to increase effectiveness, as well as have fun, and see what the students add to the lesson, too!

Also, to deepen the learning, you could start or end this lesson with a devotional time in Psalm 39:4-5, reading the verses and then asking students to write the heart response in their journals. More scripture ideas are listed in Part 1.

Notes for preparation

- Read this whole lesson first, to grasp the whole idea as well as different options.
- Gather materials ahead of time, to see how much of each of the parts you need (see notes at end—suggested amounts). Also, make sure the materials you plan to use in group time are available to students, so they can replicate this lesson easily.
- Practice this demonstration ahead of time, as this will give you a much better idea of what works best.

Part One: Jar 1

- "This container or jar represents the time we have each day—24 hours."
- "First we need sleep—we'll represent the time spent sleeping with sand. Sleep is a gift from God. 8 hours is generally considered a good amount. This is actually 1/3 of our 24 hours!" Fill sand to 1/3 of jar.
- "Then, most of us have to spend a lot of time at work. For many, that represents a very large portion of our time. Let's put in a big rock to represent that." Put in a large rock.
- "Next, think about the many small but necessary tasks that need to be done repeatedly, day after day. These are like more sand filling our days."
    - ✓ need to: Clean, clothe and feed ourselves and (for those who have children) our family,
    - ✓ clean our houses
    - ✓ do laundry
    - ✓ pay bills
    - ✓ travel
    - ✓ (add other items as students list...
- Pour sand into jar as activities are listed, about ½ to or 2/3 full.
- "We also all have other responsibilities—ministering to people outside our families, serving in the church and other ministries. This time can be symbolized by smaller rocks." Use 3/4"-1" rocks to fill the jar all the way to the top.
- "Is there anything left out of this jar, representing our time each day? Well, let's be honest!" We have had students say, 'well... we also spend too much time on things like...TV—add more medium rocks--we watch a LOT of TV! And... Facebook... we spend a lot of time on that!' [note: this discussion time should be funny—not heavy]

- "So, the jar is full! And yet we have these 3 large rocks left… and they represent the most important things in our lives." [Optional: You could ask: "What do you think these might represent?" or just go on to describe the three.]
- If we "love the Lord our God with all our heart, soul, mind, and strength (Mk 12:30)", time spent with God should be our highest priority. Time to pray and study God's Word is best done each day.
- If we are married, time with our spouse needs to be a top priority.
- If we have children, quality time with them must also be a high priority.
- "We see in our "Jar of time" that our time can be fully taken up by the things which are required to live each day, often not leaving time for the most important things. When this happens, the Holy Spirit reminds us that something is wrong. So how can we be careful (Eph 5:15) to make time for the most important things, such as "the better part" that Mary chose? (Lk 10:38-42)

Part Two: Starting Over—Jar 2

- "Let's start over with our demonstration." [empty the jar, keeping the parts separated as you place them on a large paper or plastic on the table.]
- "This empty jar still represents the time in our days. But this time we try starting with the most important parts first." Place the 3-4 large rocks in the jar; one of these should be the same rock you used to represent work. [Note: Leave gaps, don't place solidly because we want sand to filter down later.]
- "Next will come the medium rocks. – Some of the things that take our time are not the best use of our time. What are some of these? Let's set some aside and see what our day would look like with a bit less time spent watching TV, etc."
- "Next add sand." Pour carefully, shake the container as needed—note: not all the sand needs to fit back in the jar—some of the tasks can be done the next day…
- "The jar is full-- but look how differently it all fits! Our demonstration shows how prioritizing our time by what is most important helps the important parts fit better, as we ask for God's grace, strength and discernment to live to please Him each day."
- Optional: Ask a student if they want to volunteer to try the demonstration. Carefully empty the jar, making piles for the sand, rocks, etc. Help the volunteer as needed, allowing the students to add information that is left out, or add their own words—all will learn better!
- Optional after student practices: Water can also be used at the very end of the lesson, after the student practices, but be careful, sometimes the sand is actually concrete mix! ☺
- Ask, "Do you think the jar is full now?" Pour water into "full" jar. "The water is like prayer-- there is always room for prayer. Prayer, like water, flows through all the parts, enabling us to "abide" with Christ, "to walk in the Spirit" and to shine God's light to the dark world around us."
- Optional Response Time: students can take time to write in their journals, praying and asking God what He would like them to do in response to this lesson.
- Optional 1 to1 Interaction: Direct students to turn to their neighbor and discuss what they have learned from this illustration (4-5 minutes). Discuss what they feel like when they are living with "sand" first, "big rocks" last.

Optional Group Discussion: Ask, "Are there ways you can apply the truths of this demonstration to your life? What are your questions?"

End in prayer here or go on to small group time or other application activity developing your own questions.

Suggested amounts for Demonstration using a clear plastic 2-liter soda type container:
- If needed, cut top to make a wide opening
- Sand: about 3-4 cups
- Rocks about ¾"–1" size—3 cups
- 3 larger rocks (@ 2 ½ -3" in diameter)
- Water (about 3 cups)
- Cloth, paper, or plastic to protect surface.

Appendix 4: Paper People Activity

Prepare ahead of time

Fold a piece of blank paper "accordion" style. At the bottom of the page, fold about a one-inch piece up. Then flip the paper over and fold the paper up again, using your first fold as a guide for how far to fold. We want all your folds to be about the same size. Continue folding until you reach the top of the page.

Draw an outline shape of a person on the top of your first fold of paper, keeping the paper folded beneath it.

Optional: prepare one cutout of the paper people ahead of time, adding colors for clothes, faces, etc.

Demonstrate for a group

Share a verse with the students to prepare their hearts. Possible verses are Philippians 2:13 or Hebrews 10:24-25, though you can certainly use a different one of your choosing.

Talk about a vision for multiplication. As you cut out the shape you traced on your folded paper, share how God starts by equipping one person through BEE. Make sure to not cut the "hands" on the edges so that the cutouts stay together! Continue discussing that multiplication means one person's training spreads to others. As you share 2 Timothy 2:2 mandate, pull apart your shapes from the top and unfolding to the last silhouette.

Holding the string of paper people, describe the unity we experience when we study together. We are now joined together in the work God has put before us to train other students. The string of paper people all look alike, but no two people are alike. We can show this by coloring each person a little differently.

Give the students time to practice the folding, drawing, and cutting. One student could lead the group through the exercise again to help all learn more deeply.

Variations to Consider

If a group has struggled with unity, you could tear a person off of the strand and talk about the ways to reconcile and use an appropriate Scripture to encourage them. Then you can tape that person back on to the strand of cutouts to show restoration.

If the students in your group will go out in pairs to teach, you can hold up two students (still as the folded paper) to show that they can reach more students with the training as you unfold both strands.

Notes

Additional idea: Students could write names of second-generation students they have (or plan to ask, third generation, etc.) and then fold the paper dolls into one again, place it in their Bible, and take it out, open it up, to use it for praying for each of the students.

Appendix 5: A Sample Lesson Plan

The Christian Life, Lesson 1

Key Concept: The Christian life is centered on a relationship with Jesus Christ that results in obedience to His commands, love for God and other believers, and fruitfulness.

Objectives

As a result of this lesson, participants will:

- be able to describe both the central essence of the Christian life (relationship with Jesus Christ) and the characteristics of a person who is living the Christian life (obedience, love, and fruitfulness)
- be motivated to develop a more intimate relationship with Christ
- respond by evaluating their own life in terms of how centered it is on their relationship with Christ.

Introduction – 5 minutes

If you were to sum up Christianity in one word, what would that word be? According to the Bible, that word would be relationships. (Jn 17:3)

In this lesson we're going to look at the Christian Life as a relationship; this is how Jesus defined it. But it's not just any relationship; it's a particular kind of relationship. Let's look at how Jesus related to His disciples while he was here on earth, and then at some teaching that will help us understand what kind of relationship He desires to have with us.

Topic 1: Jesus' Call to His Disciples (20 minutes)

- Small group studies/reports: Look at your passage and see if you can determine what kind of relationship Jesus was inviting these prospective disciples into. What were they before Jesus called them? Immediately afterwards? Eventually?
- Mark 1:16-20 – Simon, Andrew, James, John (leave fishing, fish for men)
- Matt 9:9-10 – Matthew (leave tax collecting to follow Jesus)
- Mark 3:13-15 – first to be with him, then to go out

Topic 2: Jesus' relationship with two others (10 minutes)

- Nicodemus: John 3:1-21; 7:40-52; 19:38-42
- Zacchaeus: Luke 19:1-10
- What was Jesus' relationship with these two men? (Use a T chart to compare and contrast them) How are they alike? How are they different?

Topic 3: Signs of Discipleship (25-30 minutes)

Assign one passage to each small group) (10 minutes group work; 5 minutes for each report)

- John 8:31-32 – Following Jesus' teaching
- John 13:34-35 – Loving one another
- John 15:1-8 – Bearing fruit – what is the fruit?
- Acts 2:42-47 – ways the early Christians related to one another and to God

Topic 4: Remaining in Christ (15 minutes)
- Question 15 (Jn 15:1-8) (Whole group facilitated discussion)
- What conditions must exist for a Christian to bear fruit? What are the variables? (The closeness of our walk with Christ, our time in His Word)
- Luke 15:11-32 – Parable of two sons. Which son had the better relationship with his father? Is it necessary to go away from Christ and live in sin for a while and then come back to really appreciate your relationship with God? (No, you need to recognize even when you are doing all the "right" things you are still a sinner who needs a Savior)
- Ephesians 1:1-14 – what is the natural outflow of being in union with Christ? (Q17)
- The Lordship of Christ (Q18). Romans 10:9; Philippians 2:9-11; Colossians 2:6
- Q19 (Life Notebook): ask a student to share his answer

Topic 5: An Eternal Relationship (Q22) (15 minutes)

Write verses below on the white board; have individuals write truths taught in these verses beside them (15 minutes)
- John 14:1-3; 2 Cor 5:1-9; Phil 1:21-23; 1 Thess. 4:13-14; Rev. 21:1-3

Conclusion/Application (5 minutes)
- Having studied all these Scriptures, how would you define "relationship" as it relates to the Christian life?

Are you experiencing this kind of relationship with Christ and other believers? What could you do to make it better?

Appendix 6: BEE Curriculum

The BEE World curriculum consists of essential courses designed to equip pastors and church leaders who desire to grow in their faith and advance the cause of Christ by building faithful disciples more deeply committed to the Lord Jesus Christ and to training others, developing as Christian leaders who can lead others in strengthening churches, and gaining a deeper biblical and theological understanding of God's Word so that they can teach and train others well.

LEVEL 1 Foundations of Ministry

Purpose: To equip pastors and Christian leaders with foundational knowledge, character qualities, and skills to walk closely with the Lord and to prepare them to train others. 2 Ti 2:2.

Skill Development: Multiplying Servant Leaders, Units 1 & 2

Course Work

- Galatians
- The Christian Life
- Following the Master (Gospel of Mark)
- Studying the Bible *OR* Bible Study Methods
- Christian Marriage
- Level 1 Elective

Level 1 Electives

- One-to-One
- Character of God

LEVEL 2 Christian Leadership Development

Purpose: To equip experienced pastors and Christian leaders to serve and lead the local church and to multiply servant leaders in the body of Christ. Eph 4:11-12

Skill Development: Multiplying Servant Leaders: Unit 3

Course Work

- Colossians
- Church Dynamics
- Romans
- Leadership Training
- Daniel
- Preaching God's Word
- Level 2/3 Electives (see below Level 3 Course Work)

Level 3 Biblical & Theological Enrichment

Purpose: To equip dedicated pastors and leaders with a deeper knowledge of God's Word to accurately teach and train other believers. 2 Ti 2:15

Skill Development: Multiplying Servant Leaders: Unit 4

Course Work

- Doctrine 1
- Doctrine 2
- Advanced Studies in the Old Testament 1
- Worshipping God in the Psalms
- Elective from Level 2/3
- Elective from Level 2/3

Electives for Level 2 and 3

- Sharing God's Stories
- Life of Christ, Volumes 1 and 2
- 1 Corinthians
- The Epistle of Hebrews
- Revelation
- The Christian Family
- Introduction to Missions
- Advanced New Testament Studies
- Advanced Old Testament Studies, Volume 2

Appendix 7: Suggested Training Schedules

Important Note: Whatever training schedule is used, the beginning and ending of a course schedule should be very clearly stated. It should be workable for *all* students, and each student needs to be able to commit to it.

Weekly Sessions

Students meet for an Orientation Session for the course followed by weekly sessions based on the number of lessons. A course with twelve lessons would require thirteen sessions. The time for each weekly session should be between two and three hours.

Bi-weekly Sessions

Students meet for an Orientation Session for the course followed by sessions held every two weeks. Ideally, two lessons should be covered in each session with a meeting lasting from five to six hours. Use small groups between sessions as described below under the monthly schedule.

Monthly Sessions

Students meet for a weekend Orientation Session followed by monthly weekend sessions for ten to twelve hours to cover three or four lessons. This could be accomplished by meeting on a Friday evening (three to four hours) and on Saturday (seven to eight hours).

In addition, the group should be divided into smaller groups (three or four people) to meet together at least once or twice for two to three hours between the monthly weekend sessions. The purpose of the smaller groups is for accountability in study, discussion of key issues/study projects, and prayer together. These groups are very critical for faithful study and completion of the course.

Intensive Sessions

Students meet together for a four-to-six-day intensive time to study the course. The value of these times is that there are fewer distractions, enabling the course to be completed, and there is a deepening of relationships among the students and facilitator. This intensive session should be preceded by a one-to-two-day Orientation Session one or two month before the major intensive session. During this time the students are oriented to the course to be studied. In addition, the students should work through Lessons 1 and 2 during this session. The facilitator would then lead the students in discussion through these two lessons based on their study. This will give the students a good start on the course and give them confidence for their continued study of the course!

Also, at the Orientation Session divide the group into smaller groups of three or four persons to meet at least once every two weeks for two to three hours over the months prior to the longer intensive session. The purpose for the smaller groups is for accountability in study, discussion of key issues/study projects, and prayer together. These groups are very critical for faithful study of the material. You want all the students to come to the intensive session with their work completed!

At the four-to-six-day intensive, the rest of the lessons for the course can be discussed, led by the facilitator. Ideally at that time another course could be introduced to the students and plans made to meet one to two months later following the same format.

Another option for the intensive would be to divide the study of a course into two intensive periods, covering half of the course each time. A one-to-two-day orientation would still be needed as described above. Of course, there may be other variations of the intensive session that would better fit your situation.

Appendix 8: A Sample Training Plan and Template

Name: __John Smith_____ Date prepared: __1/2/2018_____

Goals and Objectives

Long-range goal: By the end of 2028, a total of 1600 servant leaders will have been trained by my team and those we train, through 3 generations.

Short-term objective: By the end of 2018 I and my team will have begun directly training 20 individuals (1st generation)

Medium-range objective 1: By the end of 2022 I and my team will have trained 16 faithful men (1st gen), who will be training 200 others (2nd gen)

Medium-range objective 2: By the end of 2026, I, my team, and those we have trained (1st gen) will have trained 160 faithful men (2nd gen), who will be training 2000 others (3rd gen).

Plans

Courses we will offer: All 3 levels of the BEE Curriculum

Who we will train: 1st generation: Pastors, key lay leaders, and missionaries from the 10 churches in the district I oversee, as well as several overseers from other districts.

Where we will offer training: Grace Church

Other steps we will take: Explore partnership with the church planting mission our missionaries are serving with

Action Steps and Schedule

We will complete initial preparations by 2/1/2018

We will begin recruiting and screening potential trainees on 2/1/2018

We will have materials ready for the first few training sessions by 3/1/2018

We will have our introductory meeting with our trainees on 3/5/2018

We will meet ~~weekly~~ / monthly / quarterly thereafter for 1 days each time (Saturdays)

We will study 3 courses each year, which will enable our first generation to

complete Level 1 by end of 2021

complete Level 2 by end of 2024

complete Level 3 by end of 2028

> Note: each level requires 2-3 years to complete

Our 1st generation students will start their own (2nd generation) groups by 2021

Our 2nd generation students will start their own (3rd generation) groups by 2024

Budgeting

Needs Resources		How the need will be met
People:		
Trainers	2	myself, pastor Joe
Logistics	1	Debbie, my assistant
Cooks	4	members of my church
Clean-up	4	members of my church
Other:		choose class monitor from students
Money:		
For materials	$5/book	ask students to pay for them
For facilities	$50/session	for heating ask my church to donate
For equipment	$100	ask Christian businessman to donate
For travel	none for me; student cost varied;	ask students and/or their churches to pay
For meals	$50/session	to be donated by my church
Stuff:		
Materials	printed	by the same printer we use for church materials
Facilities	large classroom	already part of our church facility
Equipment	tables, chairs	buy tables; can use chairs we already have

My BEE Training Plan

Name:_____ Date prepared: _____

Goals and Objectives

Long-range goal: By the end of 20____ a total of _____ servant leaders will have been trained by my team and those we train, through 3 generations.

Short-term objective: By the end of 20____ I and my team will have begun directly training _____ individuals (1st generation)

Medium-range objective 1: By the end of 20____ I and my team will have trained _____ faithful men (1st gen), who will be training _____ others (2nd gen)

Medium-range objective 2: By the end of 20____ I, my team, and those we have trained (1st gen) will have trained _____ faithful men (2nd gen), who will have trained _____ others (3rd gen).

Plans

Courses we will offer:

Who we will train:

Where we will offer training:

Other steps we will take:

Action Steps and Schedule

We will complete initial preparations by _____ (date)

We will begin recruiting and screening potential trainees on _____ (date)

We will have materials ready for the first few training sessions by _____ (date)

We will have our introductory meeting with our trainees on _____ (date)

We will meet weekly / monthly / quarterly thereafter for _____ days each time (circle one)

We will study _____ courses each year, which will enable our first generation to

complete Level 1 by _____

complete Level 2 by _____

complete Level 3 by _____

Note: each level requires 2-3 years to complete

Our 1st generation students will start their own (2nd generation) groups by _____

Our 2nd generation students will start their own (3rd generation) groups by _____

Budgeting

Needs Resources		How the need will be met
People:		
Trainers		
Logistics		
Cooks		
Clean-up		
Other:		
Money:		
For materials		
For facilities		
For equipment		
For travel		
For meals		
Stuff:		
Materials		
Facilities		
Equipment		

Appendix 9: Evaluating Your Training

Take fifteen to thirty minutes to make this evaluation. Answer each question with a *yes* or *no*. After answering all the questions, review the ones that you feel need some attention. Summarize any helpful changes or areas that need to be strengthened. Involve your whole group in the evaluation. They will give you some helpful feedback, plus they will learn more about evaluating their own work.

Preparation

Did I prepare adequately?

Are there ways I should prepare differently?

General Atmosphere

Did we start and end on time?

Was the meeting place adequate?

Was there a good spirit and stimulating fellowship among the group?

Did we have an adequate time for prayer? Songs?

Are there other related areas that need attention?

Student Records

Were all the students present and on time?

Did all students complete their lessons and assignments?

Did I record the needed information?

Do I need to talk with any students about completing work or being absent?

Facilitating the Lessons

Did I prepare a lesson plan for each lesson?

Did I follow my lesson plan?

Did I use my time well?

Did I cover the lesson objectives?

Did the questions generate good discussion?

Did discussion lead to better understanding of key issues?

Did discussion lead to good application?

Was everyone involved in the discussion?

Was I open to share from my own life?

Were creative teaching methods helpful?

Did the students ask questions I need to answer at the next session?

Were there any problems with the exam?

Mentoring Students

    Am I giving good attention to this area?

    Did I plan time for the students to develop as facilitators?

    Did we evaluate together their facilitating and lesson-plan development?

    Have I given students the opportunity to facilitate a lesson to the whole group?

Closing the Session

    Did I do an evaluation?

    Did I review the assignments for the next session?

    Did I review dates, time, and place as needed?

    Did I leave adequate time for prayer?

    Did I ask someone to assist me with facilitating the next session?

    Is there any student who needs some special attention?

A Summary of Areas to Be Strengthened and/or Helpful Changes

Appendix 10: Report Forms and Links

Second-generation Group Report Form

Updated April 4, 2016

Date: _____

Name(s) of Co-leader(s): _____

_____

Your First-generation Group: _____

PART ONE

Have you started a second-generation group? ___ Yes ___ No

If so, what was the start date? _____

How many students are in your second-generation group? _____

How many men are in your group? _____

How many women are in your group? _____

What are you studying in your second-generation group? _____

_____

_____

How many times have you met? _____

How often do you meet? _____

PART TWO

If you have not started a second-generation group, what is hindering you from doing so?

What problems have you encountered?

What questions do you have?

Other comments

Multiple Generation Groups Report Form

(To be introduced after 2nd generation groups have been fully established, and replaces Second Generation Groups Report Form)

Date: _____

Name (Individual filling out this form): _____

Co-leader(s)

Name of your trainer(s): _____

How many groups have you started? _____

How many students (total) are in your 2nd generation groups? _____

How many men are in your groups? _____

How many women are in your groups? _____

What are your 2nd generation groups studying? ____ The entire BEE curriculum

 ____ Selected courses (Please specify):

How many 3rd generation groups have those you trained started? _____

How many students (total) are in your 3rd generation groups? _____

How many men are in your 3rd generation groups? _____

How many women are in your 3rd generation groups? _____

What are your 3rd generation groups studying? ____ The entire BEE curriculum

 ____ Selected courses (Please specify):

PART TWO

If those you trained have not started 3rd-generation groups, what is hindering them from doing so?

What problems have you encountered in developing a multiplying training system?

What questions do you have?

Other comments

Field Ministry Forms

If you have access to BEE's SharePoint, you can download these forms directly. If you don't have access, ask your BEE Facilitator or Country Director for the files.

BEE ToolBox: *Team Site > Field Ministry > BEE ToolBox*

Student Information System Report Template: *Team Site > Field Ministry > BEE World Forms*

Instructions for filling out the Student Information System Report and a filled-out sample follow. There is also detailed instructions for data entry. You should use the BEE World Spreadsheet if it is available. Check with your first-generation facilitator to obtain a copy. If you don't have the spreadsheet, you can copy the page that has the blank form and use it.

Instructions for entering your group's data.
1. Fill out all the information in the heading area.
2. Enter the student ID that has been assigned to that student (see note for column A).
3. Enter the name and gender for each student. You can copy and paste from a previous trip.
4. Enter a "Y" into each day the student attended.
5. Enter a percentage to indicate how much homework the student completed.
6. Enter the grade the student earned for any exams given.
7. If you require class participation, verse memorization, etc. fill in the description of the work, and a numerical grade.
8. If this is the last seminar for a course, enter a "Y" to indicate that the student passed the course and a date (columns X-Y).
9. If this is the last seminar for a course, enter the course grade in column Z. This grade is at your discretion and should be based on all seminars for each course.
10. Use column "AA" for any notes for the students.

Data Entry Tool

Country	India
Language	Hindi
Region	Kullu
Group	Kullu-1
Leader	Merrikay
Generation	1

Seminar Date	3/1/2017
Course	Bible Study Methods
Seminar #	2
Facilitator	Anita
Co-Facilitator	Penny
Number of Days	4

Did the group graduate this trip? N Y/N

Use Y for Each day attended
Passed
Dropped

Grade Calculation
- 30 Attendance
- 30 Homework
- 20 Exams
- 20 Other

Other Required Work: Share Testimony

Enter the percentage each part of the course represents for the seminar grade. Please make sure that they add up to 100%.

Student Records

Student ID	Name	Alias	Gender	DROP	Att 1	Att 2	Att 3	Att 4	S(	Grd Pts	HW % Comp	HW Grd Pts	Ex1	Ex2	Ex3	Ex4	Exam Grd Pts	Other Description	Other Grade	Other Grd Pts	Seminar Grade	Pass	Final Date	Final Grade	Notes
	Pooja		F		Y	Y	Y	Y		30	100	30	100	100			20.0	Share Testimony	100	20	100.0	Y	3/5/2017	100	
	Shallini		F		Y	Y	Y	Y		30	100	30	100	100			20.0	Share Testimony	100	20	100.0	Y	3/5/2017	100	
	Kamlesh		F		Y	Y	Y	Y		30	100	30	100	100			20.0	Share Testimony	100	20	88.0	Y	3/5/2017	98	
	Bimla		F		Y	Y	Y	Y		22.5	85	25.5	100	100			20.0	Share Testimony	100	20	92.0	Y	3/5/2017	95	
	Deepa		F		Y	Y	Y	Y		30	80	24	100	80			18.0	Share Testimony	100	20	92.0	Y	3/5/2017	85	
	Jasmine		F	Y	Y	Y				7.5	50	15	0	0			0.0	Share Testimony	0	0	22.5				Attended first day then fell ill. I spoke to her sister, Bimla, who told me she would be dropping from the group.
	Meera		F		Y	Y	Y	Y		22.5	65	19.5	80	75			15.5	Share Testimony	100	20	77.5				
	Meena		F		Y	Y	Y	Y		30	80	24	80	50			13.0	Share Testimony	100	20	87.0	Y	3/5/2017	85	
	Sunita		F		Y	Y	Y	Y		30	100	30	100	100			20.0	Share Testimony	100	20	100.0	Y	3/5/2017	100	
	Vidya		F		Y	Y	Y	Y		30	80	24	0	0			0.0	Share Testimony	100	20	74.0				
										0		0					0.0			0	0.0				
										0		0					0.0			0	0.0				
										0		0					0.0			0	0.0				
										0		0					0.0			0	0.0				
										0		0					0.0			0	0.0				
										0		0					0.0			0	0.0				
										0		0					0.0			0	0.0				
										0		0					0.0			0	0.0				
										0		0					0.0			0	0.0				

Notes (callouts):

- The student ID is a distinct number that will stay with the student the whole time he or she is a student with BEE. Leave blank the first time that your group meets. The office will send you each student's ID number after your first meeting. From that time forward, you will need to enter that number in this column.
- The Attendance Grade Points is calculated based on the number of days for the seminar and the percentage specified for Attendance, both in the header section.
- Homework points are based on the amount of homework completed. Enter the percentage of homework completed. The percentage specified for Homework in the header is applied to what you enter.
- The Exam Grade points is calculated as an average of the grades listed and the Exams percentage specified in the header.
- The Project Grade Points is calculated from the score you enter and the Other percentage specified in the header. Enter the description of the work in this header.
- Seminar Grade is a total of: Attendance Grade Points, Homework Grade Points, Exam Grade Points, and Other Grade Points. This is a grade for this seminar only. The facilitator will give the Final Course Grade (column Z).
- The final grade and indication of passing the course is at the facilitator's discretion. The attendance and seminar grades should be taken into consideration and the grade given after the last seminar for the course.
- Notes: (This field will expand automatically)

Student Information System Template

Country
Language
Region
Group
Leader
Generation

Seminar Date
Course
Seminar #
Facilitator
Co-Facilitator
Number of Days

BEE World Records

Did the group graduate this trip?
☐ Y/N

Use 'Y' for Each day attended
Pass
Dropped

Grade Calculation
Attendance
Homework
Exams
Other

Other Required Work

Enter the percentage each part of the course represents for the seminar grade. Please make sure that they add up to 100%

Student Records

Student ID	Name	Gender	DROP	Attendance 1	2	3	4	5	Grd Pts	Homework % Comp	Grd Pts	Exam Grades Ex1	Ex2	Ex3	Ex4	Grd Pts	Other Description	Grade	Grd Pts	Seminar Grade	Course Pass & Date	Grade	Notes

Additional instructions for facilitators who want to keep cummulative data for their groups.

Some facilitators may want to keep this information together for each of their groups so that they can have all student records in one place. That is not difficult to do, but the responsibility for keeping these records will be the facilitators. Here are instructions for how to do that.

1. At the end of a seminar (a trip) start with a blank copy of this workbook and enter the student data into one of the seminar tabs. If you have multiple groups on one trip, enter the student data for each group into a different tab.
2. Send *this Excel Workbook* to the office with your trip report.
3. Create a *new Excel Workbook* for each group that you want to track (done only once at the beginning of a new group).
4. With both this worksheet and your group worksheet open in Excel, open the tab in this worksheet that contains the data for the group.
5. Right click on the tab at the bottom and select *Move or Copy...*
6. A dialog box will appear with your options:
    > Click on the down arrow by **To Book** and select the group worksheet you just created.
    > Select *Move to end* in the next box titled **Before Sheet**.
    > *IMPORTANT:* Click the box that says *Create a Copy*
7. Repeat this for each group you taught and for each trip. You will end up with a separate workbook for each group with the details of the student records for each seminar and course.

Made in the USA
Middletown, DE
08 September 2024

60624916R00084